MALAGA POCKET TRAVEL GUIDE 2024

Unveiling Malaga's Gems

DANIEL C. FLICK

COPYRIGHT©2024(DANIEL C. FLICK)

All intellectual property rights are retained. Without the express written permission of the publisher, no part of this book may be reproduced or transmitted in any form or by any means, electronic or mechanical, including photocopying, recording, or any information storing and retrieval system.

TABLE OF CONTENT

Scan for malaga map _____ **10**
INTRODUCTION TO MALAGA _____ **11**
   How to Use This Guide _____ 12
   Malaga at a Glance _____ 14
GETTING TO MALAGA _____ **18**
   By Air _____ 18
   By Train _____ 19
   By Road _____ 22
   Local Transport Overview _____ 24
ACCOMMODATIONS IN MALAGA _____ **28**
   Luxury Hotels _____ 28
   Mid-Range Hotels in Malaga _____ 30
   Budget Options _____ 33
   Unique Stays in Malaga _____ 36
EATING OUT IN MALAGA _____ **39**
   Traditional Andalusian Cuisine _____ 39
   Seafood Delights _____ 41
   Vegan and Vegetarian Options _____ 43
   Top 10 Must-Try Dishes _____ 45
SIGHTSEEING HIGHLIGHTS _____ **48**
   Historic Malaga _____ 48
      Alcazaba of Malaga _____ 48
      Malaga Cathedral _____ 49

Roman Theatre _____ 51

Museums and Art _____ 53
   Picasso Museum _____ 53
   Centre Pompidou Malaga _____ 55
   Carmen Thyssen Museum _____ 57

Parks and Recreation _____ 59
   Malaga Park (Parque de Malaga) _____ 59
   Montes de Malaga Natural Park _____ 61

ENTERTAINMENT AND NIGHTLIFE _____ 63

Flamenco Shows _____ 63

Nightclubs and Bars _____ 64

Family-Friendly Activities _____ 67

Live Music Venues _____ 69

7. SHOPPING _____ 72

Local Markets _____ 72

Shopping Centers _____ 74

Boutique Shops _____ 76

Souvenir Recommendations _____ 78

8. FESTIVALS AND EVENTS _____ 81

Malaga Carnival _____ 81

Holy Week (Semana Santa) _____ 83

Malaga Fair (Feria de Málaga) _____ 85

Malaga Film Festival _____ 87

9. OUTDOOR ACTIVITIES _____ 90

Beaches of Malaga _____ 90

Hiking and Biking _____ 92

Golf Courses	95
Water Sports	97

10. PRACTICAL INFORMATION _____ 101

Weather and Best Times to Visit	101
Health and Safety	103
Money and Tipping	106
Language Tips	109

11. ITINERARIES _____ 112

1 Day in Malaga	112
3 Days in Malaga	114
7 Days Exploring Costa del Sol	117

12. MAPS AND RESOURCES _____ 123

Maps of Malaga and Surrounding Areas	123
Useful Websites and Apps	125
Emergency Contacts	128

Scan for Malaga map

INTRODUCTION TO MALAGA

As I rested against the sun-warmed stone of the old Alcazaba fortress, the view before me was breathtaking. Malaga unfolded below like a vibrant quilt, alive with the buzz of daily life. In that moment, under the soft Spanish sun, I felt Malaga pull me in with its charm.

My journey started with stories of Malaga's rich history and art. They said to truly know Malaga, you need to walk its streets, meet its people, and soak in the local culture. Since it's the hometown of the famous artist Picasso, I was eager to explore the secrets and stories hidden here. Walking through the narrow streets of the city center, every corner brought a smile: balconies bursting with colorful flowers, bold murals celebrating art, and locals chatting away in cozy tapas bars.

The smell of fresh boquerones—fried fish and a local favorite—drew me to a small, busy place in a lively square. There, among the laughter and the sound of glasses clinking, I tasted dishes that were a burst of flavor: salty fish, rich olive oil, and crisp wine that seemed to carry the essence of the local vineyards. The people of Malaga, with their warm smiles, shared tales of their city—stories of old fishermen and dreaming poets.

Later, I spent an afternoon in the Picasso Museum, where each room revealed different parts of the famous artist's life. His groundbreaking art felt even more powerful here, in his birthplace. Every painting seemed to tell a personal story of his connection to Malaga.

As the day turned to evening, the city changed too. The sunset bathed the ancient Roman Theatre in a soft golden light. This old building had seen centuries pass by. Now, it watched as families and friends gathered for their evening stroll, a beloved daily ritual. I loved seeing the mix of old and new—traditional tapas bars next to trendy modern cafes, all full of people enjoying the night.

Tomorrow, I plan to visit Malaga's beautiful gardens and maybe take a trip to the Montes de Malaga Natural Park. But tonight, as I write this, the sound of a distant flamenco guitar drifts through my window. The music is full of emotion—joy and sadness mixed together. It feels like the soul of Malaga, pure and stunning.

So, I invite you to turn the page and dive deeper into this city with me. Let Malaga enchant you like it has me. In its streets, its music, and its art, there's a story waiting for you—a story of a city bathed in golden light, whispering old secrets and promising new adventures.

Malaga at a Glance

Welcome to Malaga, a gem on Spain's sunny Costa del Sol! Renowned for its seamless blend of rich history, vibrant culture, and modern amenities, Malaga offers a quintessential Mediterranean experience. Here is an expanded overview of what makes Malaga an enchanting destination for any traveler:

Geographical Location

Nestled in southern Spain, within the region of Andalusia, Malaga boasts a prime position along the famed Costa del Sol, facing the sparkling Mediterranean Sea. This coastal city enjoys a subtropical-Mediterranean climate, featuring mild winters and hot summers, perfect for year-round visits, especially by those in pursuit of sunshine and seaside leisure.

Historical Significance

Malaga's history is profound, stretching back more than 2,800 years. Originally founded by the Phoenicians, the city later became a significant part of the Roman Empire and was subsequently ruled by the Moors before being reclaimed during the Reconquista by Spanish Christian forces. Each epoch has contributed to the city's rich tapestry of cultural and architectural heritage, from Roman amphitheaters to Moorish castles.

Cultural Heritage

As the birthplace of Pablo Picasso, Malaga is a city steeped in artistic legacy. The Picasso Museum, which houses an extensive collection of his works, is a focal point for art lovers. Additionally, the Carmen Thyssen Museum and the Centre Pompidou Malaga branch reflect the city's commitment to both classic and contemporary art. Public art is also prominent here, with murals and sculptures adorning streets that pulse with creative energy.

Local Cuisine

Reflecting its coastal location, Malaga's cuisine is dominated by fresh seafood. Dishes such as 'espetos' (sardines skewered and grilled over a wood fire) and 'boquerones' (fresh anchovies marinated in vinegar or fried) are local staples. The city's numerous tapas bars provide a lively culinary scene, offering an array of traditional Andalusian dishes alongside innovative culinary creations, allowing visitors to indulge in a true taste of local flavors.

Beaches and Natural Beauty

Malaga's coastline is dotted with beautiful beaches, from bustling seafronts equipped with all necessary amenities to tranquil bays ideal for those seeking peace. The city is also a stone's throw from the Montes de Malaga Natural Park, an expansive area perfect for outdoor activities like hiking, cycling, and observing local flora and fauna. The park is an excellent spot for escaping the urban bustle and reconnecting with nature.

Festivals and Events

The cultural calendar in Malaga is vibrant and diverse. Noteworthy events include the Malaga Carnival, the dramatic and emotive Holy Week processions, and the colorful Malaga Fair. Each festival offers visitors a unique opportunity to experience local customs and enjoy the festive atmosphere filled with music, dance, and traditional costumes.

Modern Attractions

Malaga does not shy away from modernity. The city boasts sophisticated shopping centers, lush botanical gardens, and the stylish port area, Muelle Uno, which is lined with chic shops, eateries, and bars, all offering splendid views of the Mediterranean. This blend of historical charm and contemporary convenience makes Malaga a versatile destination for tourists.

Accessibility

Malaga is highly accessible, serviced by the Malaga-Costa del Sol Airport with extensive international connections. The city's public transport network is robust, featuring buses, trains, and a metro line, facilitating easy exploration of both the city's heart and the enchanting regions beyond.

Why Visit?

Malaga is far more than just a launchpad to the Costa del Sol; it's a city vibrant with life, steeped in culture and history, graced with delightful weather, and radiating a welcoming atmosphere. Whether you are keen to delve into the world of art, relax on the beach, explore historical sites, or savor the local gastronomy, Malaga offers a rich blend of experiences that cater to all preferences.

GETTING TO MALAGA

By Air

Malaga is highly accessible from virtually anywhere in the world thanks to the Malaga-Costa del Sol Airport, one of the busiest airports in Spain. Located just 8 kilometers southwest of the city center, it serves as the main international gateway for travelers heading to the Costa del Sol. Here's what you need to know about arriving in Malaga by air:

1. Airport Overview: Malaga-Costa del Sol Airport (IATA: AGP) features three terminals, with Terminal 3 being the most modern and handling the majority of international flights. The airport is well-equipped with a variety of services including duty-free shops, a wide range of eateries, car rental agencies, and free WiFi.

2. Flight Connectivity: The airport offers extensive flight options with direct connections to over 60 countries. Major airlines, including low-cost carriers, operate regular flights to and from major cities across Europe, as well as seasonal long-haul flights to the United States, Canada, the Middle East, and North Africa.

3. Getting to and from the Airport:

- By Train: The airport is served by the C1 line of the suburban train system (Cercanías), which connects it with central Malaga in about 12 minutes. The train station is conveniently located just a short walk from Terminal 3.

- By Bus: Several bus lines operate between the airport and various points in Malaga and the surrounding areas. The Express Line A connects the airport with the city center, providing a quick and economical option for travelers.

- By Taxi: Taxis are available outside the arrivals area of each terminal. They offer a convenient, although more costly, way to reach your destination. Official taxis should be used to avoid overcharging.

- By Car Rental: Numerous car rental agencies have offices at the airport, allowing for easy booking and pick-up. Driving from the airport to the city center typically takes about 15 to 20 minutes, depending on traffic.

4. Tips for a Smooth Arrival:

- Check the airport website for live flight information and terminal details.

- Consider pre-booking your airport transfer, especially if you arrive late at night.

- Be aware of taxi surcharges that apply during night hours and on holidays.

- If you plan to explore the region by car, studying a map or using a GPS can help navigate the area more comfortably.

Arriving in Malaga by air is straightforward and convenient, making it an ideal starting point for your adventures in the city and beyond. Whether you're coming for the sunny beaches, the rich culture, or the lively festivals, Malaga is just a flight away.

By Train

Traveling to Malaga by train is a convenient and enjoyable option for visitors coming from other parts of Spain or neighboring European countries. Malaga's Maria Zambrano Railway Station is a major hub that connects the city not only to Spain's extensive high-speed rail network but also to other traditional regional and national services. Here's what you need to know about arriving in Malaga by train:

1. Station Overview: Malaga Maria Zambrano Station is centrally located and offers various amenities to facilitate a comfortable transit. It includes a shopping center, numerous eateries, car rental services, and tourist information. The station is also integrated with the local bus and metro services, making it a convenient point from which to explore the city.

2. High-Speed Trains (AVE): The AVE (Alta Velocidad Española) high-speed train connects Malaga with major cities such as Madrid, Barcelona, and Seville. The journey from Madrid to Malaga can be as short as 2.5 hours, making it an excellent option for quick and comfortable travel. The AVE trains are known for their punctuality, speed, and modern facilities, including WiFi.

3. Other Trains: In addition to the high-speed services, Malaga is accessible via other slower regional trains and long-distance trains. These are more economical options and connect Malaga to a wider array of destinations across Spain, although travel times will be longer compared to the AVE.

4. International Connections: For travelers coming from other European countries, it's possible to connect to Spain's AVE network via France. The SNCF-TGV (French Railways) operates direct high-speed trains to Barcelona, from where passengers can transfer to a Spanish high-speed train to Malaga.

5. Getting to and from the Station:

- By Bus: Numerous city bus lines serve the station, allowing easy access to different parts of Malaga and the suburbs.

- By Metro: Maria Zambrano Station is also a stop on the Malaga Metro, providing fast and efficient service to various city locations.

- By Taxi: A taxi rank is located just outside the station. Taxis offer a convenient way to reach your final destination, especially if you're traveling with lots of luggage.

6. Tips for Train Travel:

- Book your tickets in advance, especially if you plan to travel by AVE, as seats can be limited during peak travel times and fares tend to rise closer to the departure date.

- Check if your train ticket allows you to use local public transport in Malaga for free within a certain time frame of your arrival.

- If arriving late, ensure you have pre-arranged transport or accommodation as local transport services may be less frequent at night.

Traveling to Malaga by train offers a scenic, efficient, and relaxing alternative to flying. Whether you are zipping across the country on a high-speed train or meandering through the Spanish countryside on a regional service, the train journey can be an enriching part of your travel experience.

By Road

Arriving in Malaga by road is a popular choice for travelers who prefer the flexibility and freedom of driving. Whether you're navigating the scenic routes of Spain's Costa del Sol in a rental car or arriving by bus, the roads to Malaga offer breathtaking views and straightforward connections. Here's a detailed guide for those planning to reach Malaga by road:

1. Driving to Malaga: Malaga is well-connected to the rest of Spain through an extensive network of highways and motorways. The main artery leading into the city is the A-7 (Autovía del Mediterráneo), which runs along the Mediterranean coast, connecting Malaga to other major coastal towns like Marbella and Torremolinos, as well as to cities such as Barcelona and Valencia. The A-45 highway connects Malaga to Cordoba and, further north, to Madrid.

- Scenic Routes: If you have time and prefer scenic drives, consider taking some of the coastal roads that offer stunning sea views and access to smaller towns and villages.

- Toll Roads: Some routes, like parts of the A-7, have toll sections. Be prepared to pay tolls or plan your route to avoid them if preferred.

- Parking in Malaga: Once in Malaga, finding parking can be challenging, especially in the city center. It's advisable to use monitored parking lots or garages to avoid fines and to secure your vehicle.

2. By Bus: Malaga is also accessible by long-distance buses from major cities across Spain and Europe. The main bus station in Malaga is located near the Maria Zambrano Train Station, providing convenient access to public transport and taxis.

- National and International Bus Services: Companies like ALSA and Avanza offer frequent routes from cities like Madrid, Seville, and Barcelona. International routes vary by season but generally include connections from cities in Portugal, France, and beyond.

- Comfort and Convenience: Modern long-distance buses are equipped with amenities such as air conditioning, restrooms, free WiFi, and power outlets, ensuring a comfortable journey.

3. Car Rentals: If you're flying into Malaga and plan to travel by road throughout your stay, numerous car rental agencies are available at the Malaga-Costa del Sol Airport and throughout the city. Renting a car gives you the liberty to explore the region at your own pace.

4. Tips for Road Travel:

- Plan Your Route: Before you embark, plan your route and check traffic conditions. Apps like Google Maps and Waze can be invaluable for real-time navigation and traffic updates.

- Legal Requirements: Ensure you are familiar with Spanish driving laws. Car rental agencies can provide necessary documentation and equipment, such as reflective vests and warning triangles, which are required by law.

- Rest Stops: If you're embarking on a long drive, plan for adequate rest stops to avoid fatigue. The Spanish road network offers well-equipped rest areas where you can refresh and recharge.

Driving to Malaga offers a wonderful opportunity to see the Spanish landscape and explore the region's diverse attractions with ease. Whether you choose the speed of the motorways or the charm of the coastal roads, traveling by road can enhance your overall experience of discovering Spain.

Local Transport Overview

Navigating around Malaga is straightforward thanks to its comprehensive and efficient public transportation system. Whether you prefer buses, trains, or more personalized options like taxis and bike rentals, Malaga offers a variety of transport modes to suit different preferences and needs. Here's an updated overview of the local transport available in Malaga, including prices and pick-up point locations:

1. Buses: Malaga's bus network, operated by EMT (Empresa Malagueña de Transporte), covers the entire city and its suburbs, including direct routes to popular tourist areas along the coast.

- City Buses: Regular services cover all major districts and points of interest. Buses are frequent, affordable (around €1.30 per trip), and equipped with air conditioning. Major bus stops include Alameda Principal and the Maria Zambrano Train Station.

- Night Buses: Several night bus routes operate, although less frequently. Fares are similar to daytime services.

- Tourist Bus: The hop-on hop-off tourist buses cost around €18 for a day pass, providing audio-guided tours and stopping at major attractions. Tickets can be purchased on the bus or at major tourist spots.

2. Metro: Malaga's metro system is a clean, fast, and efficient way to travel, especially useful for reaching destinations outside the immediate city center:

- Routes: There are two metro lines, L1 and L2, that connect the city center with the western and southwestern residential areas. Single trips start at €1.35, with day passes available.

- Pick-up Points: Major stations include El Perchel/Maria Zambrano (connected to the main train station) and Malagueta.

3. Trains (Cercanías): The commuter rail service connects Malaga with nearby towns and cities:

- C1 Line: Runs between Malaga Centro-Alameda and Malaga Airport, continuing to Fuengirola. A single trip to the airport costs about €1.80.

- C2 Line: Connects Malaga with inland towns. Fares vary depending on distance, starting from €1.80.

- Major Station: Malaga Centro-Alameda, located centrally and accessible from most parts of the city.

4. Taxis: Taxis can be hailed on the street, booked via phone, or through various smartphone apps:

- Rates: Metered, with a base fare of around €3.50, plus €1 per additional kilometer. There are extra charges for airport trips (about €5 extra) and nighttime rides.
- Pick-up Points: Readily available at taxi stands throughout the city, especially near tourist areas, hotels, and the Maria Zambrano Train Station.

5. Bicycles and Electric Scooters: With its mostly flat terrain and growing network of bike lanes, cycling and scooter rides are popular:

- Bike Rentals: Shops and automated rental stations around the city offer bikes for around €10 per day. Major pick-up points include the city center and near the beach.
- Scooter Rentals: Electric scooters can be rented through app-based sharing services, with prices starting at €1 to unlock plus €0.15 per minute.

6. Car Rentals: Car rental agencies are found within the city and at the airport. Daily rental rates start at about €25, depending on the vehicle type.

- Pick-up Points: Mainly at Malaga-Costa del Sol Airport and major hotels.

7. Walking: Many of Malaga's attractions are concentrated in the city center, making walking a pleasant and practical option. Key

pedestrian areas include the historic city center and the Malagueta district.

Tips for Using Local Transport:

- Multi-Use Cards: Purchase a rechargeable transport card (Tarjeta Monedero) for convenience and discounted fares on buses and metro.

- Apps and Maps: Use transport apps and city maps to plan routes efficiently.

- Timetables and Frequency: Check timetables, especially for night services and public holidays, to ensure smooth travel plans.

With these detailed insights into prices and pick-up points, visitors to Malaga can efficiently plan their transportation, ensuring a smooth and enjoyable experience while exploring the city.

ACCOMMODATIONS IN MALAGA

Luxury Hotels

When you visit Malaga and seek a touch of luxury, you have several exquisite hotels to choose from. These establishments are renowned for their superior service and facilities and are conveniently located, allowing you to fully enjoy everything the city has to offer. Here's a closer look at some of the top luxury hotels in Malaga, including their locations, amenities, prices, and star ratings:

1. Gran Hotel Miramar GL

- Location: Nestled in the prestigious La Caleta neighborhood, this hotel offers stunning views of the Mediterranean Sea.

- Description: The Gran Hotel Miramar GL exudes historical charm with modern luxury. Its façade and interiors are beautifully restored, reflecting the grandeur of early 20th-century architecture.

- Amenities: You can enjoy various dining options, a world-class spa, an outdoor pool, and access to a private beach area.

- Prices: Expect rooms to start from €250 per night.

- Star Rating: 5-star

2. Vincci Selección Posada del Patio

- Location: This hotel is right in the heart of Malaga, close to both the Malaga Cathedral and the Picasso Museum.

- Description: Known for blending historical elements with contemporary comfort, this hotel incorporates remnants of Malaga's ancient city walls within its structure.

- Amenities: Enjoy a rooftop pool with breathtaking city views, a reputable restaurant, a library, and luxurious rooms equipped with modern amenities.

- Prices: Average nightly rates are around €180.

- Star Rating: 5-star

3. Room Mate Valeria

- Location: Ideally placed near the Port of Malaga and just a short stroll from the Picasso Museum.

- Description: This boutique hotel captivates with its vibrant and colorful interior design, inspired by the local Andalusian culture.

- Amenities: Features include a rooftop bar and pool, stylish rooms with designer furnishings, and a fitness center.

- Prices: Rooms start at approximately €150 per night.

- Star Rating: 4-star

4. Parador de Málaga Gibralfaro

- Location: Positioned on a hilltop next to the Gibralfaro Castle, it offers panoramic views of Malaga city and the coast.

- Description: As part of the renowned Parador chain, this hotel blends traditional Spanish architecture with modern comforts in a historical or natural setting.

- Amenities: Includes a seasonal swimming pool, a celebrated restaurant specializing in local cuisine, and spacious rooms with terraces.

- Prices: Nightly rates begin at around €200.

- Star Rating: 4-star

5. Hotel Molina Lario

- Location: Situated directly across from the Cathedral of Malaga in the historic city center.

- Description: A chic hotel that merges two renovated buildings with a new structure, offering a perfect mix of historical architecture and modern luxury.

- Amenities: Features a rooftop pool and terrace with cathedral views, a contemporary restaurant, and elegant rooms.

- Prices: Starting from about €170 per night.

- Star Rating: 4-star

These luxury hotels in Malaga not only provide a place to stay but also enhance your travel experience with their unique features, catering to diverse preferences whether you are drawn to historic environments, modern design, or stunning vistas.

Mid-Range Hotels in Malaga

For a balance of comfort and cost, mid-range hotels in Malaga offer excellent accommodations without the premium price tag of luxury hotels. These hotels provide great amenities, convenient locations, and are perfect for travelers looking for quality lodging that won't break the bank. Here are some of the best mid-range hotel options in Malaga, complete with locations, amenities, and approximate pricing:

1. Hotel del Pintor

- Location: Situated in the heart of Malaga's historic center, close to the Picasso Museum and the vibrant Plaza de la Merced.

- Description: This boutique hotel is themed around the concept of an artist's workshop, with unique, colorful decor and a contemporary feel.

- Amenities: Offers free Wi-Fi, a lounge area, personalized customer service, and complimentary city tours.

- Prices: Nightly rates start at around €90.

- Star Rating: 3-star

2. Mariposa Hotel Malaga

- Location: Located on a quiet street but just a short walk from the shopping streets of Calle Larios and the Carmen Thyssen Museum.
- Description: Known for its stylish, Art Deco-inspired interiors and welcoming atmosphere.
- Amenities: Features include a rooftop terrace, a cozy bar, room service, and spacious, well-appointed rooms.
- Prices: Prices begin at about €100 per night.
- Star Rating: 4-star

3. Hotel Soho Bahía Málaga

- Location: Perfectly positioned in the Soho district, known for its art and culture, close to the Contemporary Art Center.
- Description: The hotel reflects the artistic flair of its neighborhood with modern design and artistic decorations.
- Amenities: Guests can enjoy a cafeteria, a sun terrace, meeting facilities, and rooms equipped with modern conveniences.
- Prices: Starting at approximately €85 per night.
- Star Rating: 3-star

4. Hotel Zenit Malaga

- Location: Located in the quieter, residential area of Malaga, but still within easy access to the city center via public transport.

- Description: Offers a comfortable and relaxed setting with a focus on hospitality and service.
- Amenities: Features include a restaurant serving Mediterranean cuisine, a business center, and contemporary rooms with free Wi-Fi.
- Prices: Room rates start from about €75 per night.
- Star Rating: 3-star

5. Sercotel Malaga

- Location: Close to the Malaga train station and just a short walk from the main shopping and dining areas of the city.
- Description: This hotel is ideal for both leisure and business travelers, offering a comfortable stay with all the necessary amenities.
- Amenities: Includes a restaurant, gym facilities, conference rooms, and soundproofed rooms for a restful night's sleep.
- Prices: Average prices are around €95 per night.
- Star Rating: 4-star

These mid-range hotels in Malaga ensure you enjoy a comfortable stay with good service and convenient access to the city's main attractions, making them an excellent choice for budget-conscious travelers who still seek quality and convenience.

Budget Options

For travelers keeping a close eye on their budget, Malaga offers a variety of affordable accommodations that don't compromise on comfort and accessibility. These budget-friendly options provide essential amenities and a convenient base from which to explore the city. Here are some of the top budget accommodations in Malaga, including details about their locations, amenities, and pricing:

1. Ibis Budget Málaga Centro

- Location: Centrally located, just a short walk from Malaga's main attractions, including the Carmen Thyssen Museum and the bustling Calle Larios.

- Description: This hotel offers straightforward, modern rooms specifically designed for the budget-conscious traveler.

- Amenities: Guests can enjoy free Wi-Fi, a breakfast buffet, and 24-hour reception services.

- Prices: Room rates start from as low as €50 per night.

- Star Rating: 1-star

2. Hostel Bellavista Playa Malaga

- Location: Situated right on the beachfront, offering stunning views of the sea, and is perfect for those who prefer a more relaxed setting.

- Description: A popular choice among backpackers and budget travelers, this hostel features both private rooms and shared dormitories.

- Amenities: Includes access to a communal kitchen, a lounge area, and free Wi-Fi. Activities such as beach volleyball and yoga sessions are often organized.

- Prices: Dorm beds start at around €20 per night, with private rooms costing slightly more.

- Star Rating: Hostel

3. Hotel Domus

- Location: Located in the quieter Pedregalejo area, known for its beaches and traditional fish restaurants, yet only a short bus ride from the city center.

- Description: A small and stylish hotel that offers a more intimate and personalized experience.

- Amenities: Features a rooftop terrace, a café, and modern rooms equipped with air conditioning and free Wi-Fi.

- Prices: Prices begin at about €40 per night.

- Star Rating: 1-star

4. Feel Hostels Soho Malaga

- Location: Ideally placed in the heart of the Soho district, known for its artistic vibe and proximity to cultural sites.

- Description: This hostel is favored for its lively atmosphere and colorful interiors, appealing mainly to younger travelers and backpackers.

- Amenities: Offers a kitchen, laundry facilities, a common room, and organized events like city tours and pub crawls.

- Prices: Dormitory beds start from around €18 per night.

- Star Rating: Hostel

5. Pension Terminal

- Location: Situated near the central bus station, making it highly convenient for travelers exploring the wider region.

- Description: Provides simple, clean accommodations with a friendly service.

- Amenities: Features include air-conditioned rooms, free Wi-Fi, and some rooms come with private bathrooms.

- Prices: Room rates start at approximately €30 per night.

- Star Rating: 2-star

These budget-friendly options in Malaga ensure that even travelers on the tightest of budgets can enjoy a comfortable and enjoyable stay, making the most out of their visit without breaking the bank. Whether you're looking for a beachfront hostel or a centrally-located hotel, Malaga's affordable accommodations cater to all preferences.

Unique Stays in Malaga

Malaga isn't just about typical hotels; it offers some truly unique places to stay that can make your visit unforgettable. From historic buildings transformed into elegant accommodations to quirky boutique hotels, these unique stays provide more than just a place to sleep—they offer a distinct experience that reflects the charm and character of Malaga. Here's a look at some of the most unique accommodations in the city, complete with their features and amenities:

1. Castillo de Santa Catalina

    - Location: Set on a hill overlooking the Mediterranean Sea, this historic castle is just a few minutes from the city center.

    - Description: Originally built in the early 20th century, this stunning castle has been beautifully converted into a luxury boutique hotel, preserving its historic charm.

    - Amenities: Offers elegant rooms with antique furnishings, a rooftop terrace with panoramic views, and exquisite dining options.

    - Prices: Starting from €150 per night.

2. La Casa Azul - B&B + Apartments

    - Location: Located in the vibrant Soho district, close to the Contemporary Art Centre.

    - Description: Inspired by the famous blue house of Frida Kahlo, this colorful and artistically decorated B&B offers a cultural experience as vibrant as its surroundings.

    - Amenities: Guests can enjoy custom-decorated rooms, a lovely garden terrace, and homemade breakfast served daily.

    - Prices: Rooms start at around €100 per night.

3. Hotel Palacete de Alamos

    - Location: Situated in the historic center, near the Picasso Museum and Malaga Cathedral.

- Description: This 18th-century palace has been transformed into a modern hotel while retaining its original baroque architecture and classic details.

- Amenities: Features contemporary art throughout, a gourmet restaurant, and stylishly updated rooms.

- Prices: Nightly rates begin at about €130.

4. Malaga Lodge Guesthouse

- Location: Set in a quiet residential area close to the historic center.

- Description: Housed in a beautifully preserved 19th-century building, this guesthouse offers a cozy and intimate atmosphere.

- Amenities: Includes a charming garden, shared kitchen facilities, and tastefully decorated rooms with vintage touches.

- Prices: Starting from €60 per night.

5. Soho Boutique Equitativa

- Location: Located right in the heart of the city, this hotel offers easy access to Malaga's main cultural attractions.

- Description: Set in the iconic Equitativa building, which combines historical architecture with a sleek, modern design.

- Amenities: Features include rooftop views, chic decor, and proximity to major landmarks.

- Prices: Rooms start at around €110 per night.

These unique stays in Malaga are perfect for travelers seeking something out of the ordinary. Each offers a different perspective on the city's rich history and culture, providing more than just a place to rest but a memorable part of your overall experience in Malaga. Whether you're nestled in a historic castle, staying in a vibrant artist-inspired B&B, or enjoying the elegance of a restored palace, these accommodations ensure your stay is as extraordinary as the city itself.

EATING OUT IN MALAGA

Traditional Andalusian Cuisine

When it comes to dining in Malaga, exploring the traditional Andalusian cuisine is a must for an authentic culinary experience. Rich in flavors and influenced by centuries of history, Andalusian cuisine reflects the region's diverse cultural heritage and its proximity to the Mediterranean Sea. Here are some quintessential dishes and dining experiences you shouldn't miss when indulging in traditional Andalusian fare in Malaga:

1. Gazpacho:

- Description: This chilled tomato soup is a refreshing and iconic Andalusian dish, perfect for hot summer days. Made with ripe tomatoes, peppers, onions, garlic, and cucumbers, seasoned with olive oil, vinegar, and salt, gazpacho is a flavorful and healthy starter.

- Where to Try: Look for authentic gazpacho in traditional tapas bars and restaurants throughout Malaga.

2. Pescaíto Frito:

- Description: A beloved seafood dish, pescaíto frito consists of an assortment of small fish, such as anchovies, sardines, and squid, lightly battered and fried to crispy perfection. Served hot and crispy, it's a staple of Andalusian coastal cuisine.

- Where to Try: Head to beachside chiringuitos (beach bars) or seafood restaurants along the Malaga coast for the freshest pescaíto frito.

3. Espetos de Sardinas:

- Description: A Malaga specialty, espetos de sardinas are skewered sardines grilled over an open flame on traditional wooden sticks. The smoky flavor and tender texture make them a favorite among locals and visitors alike.

- Where to Try: Look for beachfront restaurants and chiringuitos along Malaga's beaches, where you can watch the sardines grilling right before your eyes.

4. Porra Antequerana:

- Description: Similar to gazpacho but with a thicker consistency, porra antequerana is a hearty cold soup made with tomatoes, bread, garlic, olive oil, and vinegar, often garnished with hard-boiled eggs and jamón serrano. It's a satisfying dish bursting with flavor.

- Where to Try: Seek out traditional taverns and family-run restaurants in Malaga's historic center for an authentic taste of porra antequerana.

5. Malaga Raisin Wine:

- Description: Malaga is renowned for its sweet fortified wine made from sun-dried Pedro Ximénez or Moscatel grapes. This indulgent dessert wine boasts rich flavors of raisins, caramel, and dried fruits, making it the perfect accompaniment to Andalusian desserts or enjoyed on its own.

- Where to Try: Visit local bodegas (wine bars) or wine shops in Malaga to sample and purchase Malaga raisin wine.

Exploring traditional Andalusian cuisine in Malaga is not just about savoring delicious dishes but also immersing yourself in the rich culinary heritage of the region. Whether you're enjoying a bowl of refreshing gazpacho, indulging in crispy pescaíto frito by the sea, or sipping on sweet Malaga raisin wine, each bite and sip is a celebration of Andalusia's vibrant food culture.

Seafood Delights

Malaga, with its long coastline and vibrant fishing heritage, is a paradise for seafood lovers. The Mediterranean and Atlantic waters provide a bountiful harvest of marine delicacies that are celebrated in local kitchens. From high-end restaurants to casual beachfront eateries, the city offers a plethora of options for enjoying fresh seafood. Here's where and what to indulge in for a truly delightful seafood experience in Malaga:

1. Mariscos (Shellfish):

- Description: Feast on a variety of shellfish including gambas (prawns), langostinos (king prawns), almejas (clams), and mejillones (mussels). Each is prepared with care, often grilled or steamed to enhance their natural flavors, and served with a squeeze of local lemon.

- Where to Try: Visit the Atarazanas Market where seafood stalls display fresh catches daily. Many local restaurants also serve these delicious shellfish either as tapas or main dishes.

2. Calamares Fritos (Fried Squid):

- Description: A staple in Malaga, these rings or whole pieces of squid are lightly breaded and deep-fried until golden. Crispy on the outside and tender on the inside, calamares are typically enjoyed with a tangy alioli sauce or simply a wedge of lemon.

- Where to Try: Calamares are ubiquitous in tapas bars throughout Malaga. For a particularly famous preparation, visit bars in the city center where the squid is fresh and expertly fried.

3. Boquerones (Anchovies):

- Description: Malaga is famous for its boquerones, either fried in a light batter (boquerones fritos) or marinated in vinegar (boquerones en vinagre). These small fish are a local delicacy, celebrated for their mild flavor and delicate texture.

- Where to Try: Look for boquerones at any seafood restaurant or tapas bar in Malaga, especially those near the coast where the catch is freshest.

4. Arroz con Mariscos (Seafood Rice):

- Description: This rich and savory dish is Spain's answer to paella and features a mix of seafood cooked with seasoned rice. Each restaurant has its own version, but common ingredients include shrimp, mussels, clams, and sometimes squid, all infused with saffron and local herbs.

- Where to Try: Seafood restaurants along the promenade offer some of the best arroz con mariscos, with views of the sea adding to the dining experience.

5. Zarzuela de Mariscos:

- Description: Zarzuela de Mariscos is a luxurious seafood stew, perfect for those who want to sample a bit of everything. This aromatic stew typically contains fish, shellfish, and crustaceans, cooked in a tomato and wine-based sauce, seasoned with garlic, onions, and Spanish paprika.

- Where to Try: Upscale seafood restaurants often feature this dish, which showcases the quality and diversity of local seafood.

Dining out in Malaga allows seafood enthusiasts to explore an array of traditional and innovative dishes, each telling a story of the region's culinary prowess and its relationship with the sea. Whether you're sipping on a chilled glass of white wine paired with fresh shellfish or digging into a hearty seafood stew, the flavors of Malaga promise a memorable gastronomic journey.

Vegan and Vegetarian Options

In recent years, Malaga has embraced the growing trend of vegetarian and vegan lifestyles, expanding its culinary repertoire to include a wide range of plant-based options. Whether you are a strict vegan, a vegetarian, or simply looking to incorporate more plant-based meals into your diet, Malaga offers a delightful array of eateries that cater to your needs. Here's a guide to some of the top vegan and vegetarian dining experiences in the city:

1. Vegetarian Tapas:

- Description: Traditional Spanish tapas bars are adapting their menus to include more vegetarian options. Dishes like patatas bravas (spicy potatoes), pimientos de padrón (fried green peppers), and berenjenas con miel (fried eggplant with honey) are must-tries.

- Where to Try: Many tapas bars around the historic city center have started offering a range of vegetarian tapas. Keep an eye out for menus that highlight vegetarian choices.

2. Vegan Restaurants:

- Description: A number of dedicated vegan restaurants have opened in Malaga, serving everything from vegan versions of traditional Spanish dishes to international cuisine like vegan burgers, sushi, and pizza.

- Where to Try: Explore areas like Soho and the historic center, where vegan restaurants offer creative and delicious plant-based meals.

3. Health Food Cafes:

- Description: These cafes not only offer vegetarian and vegan options but also focus on health-conscious meals that include superfoods, gluten-free, and organic products. Expect to find a variety of salads, smoothies, grain bowls, and homemade vegan desserts.

- Where to Try: Health food cafes are scattered throughout Malaga, particularly in trendy neighborhoods and near yoga studios and health clubs.

4. Vegetarian-Friendly International Cuisine:

- Description: With its cosmopolitan population, Malaga boasts a variety of international restaurants offering vegetarian and vegan dishes. From Italian to Middle Eastern, Asian to Mexican, there are plenty of options to explore.

- Where to Try: Look for ethnic restaurants in more diverse neighborhoods, which often have extensive vegetarian sections on their menus.

5. Local Markets and Organic Shops:

- Description: For those who prefer to cook their own meals or are looking for local vegan and vegetarian ingredients, Malaga's markets and organic shops are stocked with fresh, local produce, vegan cheeses, plant-based milks, and more.

- Where to Try: The Atarazanas Market is a good start for fresh vegetables and fruits, while specialized organic shops offer a range of vegan products.

These options reflect Malaga's growing commitment to catering to a diverse array of dietary preferences. Eating vegan or vegetarian in Malaga is not only easy but also a delightful way to explore the city's evolving food scene, ensuring that every diner can find something to suit their taste and lifestyle.

Top 10 Must-Try Dishes

When visiting Malaga, immersing yourself in the local cuisine is a journey through the region's rich culinary heritage and vibrant flavors. Here are the top 10 must-try dishes that showcase the best of Malaga's gastronomy:

1. Gazpacho or Salmorejo:

- Description: Both are traditional cold soups perfect for the warm climate. Gazpacho is a refreshing blend of tomatoes, cucumbers, peppers, onions, and garlic, while Salmorejo is thicker, creamier, and often topped with hard-boiled eggs and jamón serrano.

2. Espetos de Sardinas:

- Description: Sardines skewered and grilled over a pit of coals, a typical sight on Malaga's beaches. The fish are fresh, simple, and deliciously smoky.

3. Fritura Malagueña:

- Description: A mixed fry of local fish and seafood, including anchovies, squid, and small sole, lightly battered and fried. It's a delightful showcase of the day's catch.

4. Ajoblanco:

- Description: An almond and garlic cold soup, often served with grapes or melon. This dish is surprisingly refreshing and packed with flavor.

5. Porra Antequerana:

- Description: Similar to gazpacho, this thick tomato soup is garnished with tuna, ham, or hard-boiled eggs, providing a richer flavor profile.

6. Boquerones en Vinagre:

    - Description: Fresh anchovies marinated in vinegar and garlic, served cold. These are a staple of Malaga's tapas bars and a true taste of the sea.

7. Berenjenas con Miel:

    - Description: Slices of eggplant fried in a light batter and drizzled with local cane honey, combining sweet and savory in each bite.

8. Malaga Raisin Ice Cream:

    - Description: Ice cream made with the famous Malaga raisins, offering a sweet and creamy treat with a distinct local flavor.

9. Chivo Lechal Malagueño:

    - Description: Tender young goat meat, typically roasted or stewed, and served in towns across the Malaga province. It's a traditional dish that highlights the region's inland culinary practices.

10. Piononos de Santa Fe:

    - Description: Although originally from Granada, these small, sweet pastries have become a favorite in Malaga. They consist of a thin layer of pastry rolled into a cylinder, soaked in syrup, and topped with toasted cream.

Each of these dishes tells a story of Malaga's history, culture, and environment, making them not just meals but experiences to savor. Whether you're dining seaside, in the bustling heart of the city, or in the tranquil hills surrounding Malaga, these culinary delights are sure to enhance your visit.

SIGHTSEEING HIGHLIGHTS

Historic Malaga

Alcazaba of Malaga

- Location: Situated in the heart of Malaga, this magnificent Moorish fortress rises on a hill at the center of the city, offering expansive views of both the urban landscape and the Mediterranean Sea.

- Description: As one of Spain's most well-preserved alcazabas, the Alcazaba is a prime example of Muslim architecture, featuring robust defensive walls, enchanting gardens, ornate fountains, and palatial complexes adorned with Islamic art and architectural flourishes.

- History: Built in the early 11th century by the Hammudid dynasty, this fortress was designed to safeguard Malaga from pirates and invaders. It has been renovated multiple times through the centuries, notably during the reign of the Nasrids.

- How to Get There: You can reach the Alcazaba easily on foot from Plaza de la Merced, a brief 10-minute walk uphill. If you prefer a less strenuous route, take the elevator from Calle Guillen Sotelo straight to the entrance.

- Fares: Entry costs around €3.50 for adults. Discounts are available for children and seniors. If you're a resident of Malaga, you can enjoy free entry on Sundays after 2 PM.

- How to Explore: You have the option to wander through the Alcazaba independently or join a guided tour for a more informative experience. Audio guides are available for hire.

- Opening and Closing Hours: Open from 9:00 AM to 8:00 PM during the summer months (April to October) and from 9:00 AM to 6:00 PM during the winter months (November to March).

- Tips for Visitors:

    - Wear comfortable shoes, as you'll encounter lots of walking on uneven paths.

    - Plan your visit early in the morning or later in the afternoon to dodge the crowds and the midday heat, especially in the summer.

    - Don't miss out on the Roman Theatre right below the Alcazaba—it's free to enter and adds another dimension to Malaga's rich historical tapestry.

    - Allocate at least 1 to 2 hours to thoroughly enjoy all that the Alcazaba has to offer, from its panoramic views to its peaceful gardens.

Visiting the Alcazaba offers you a captivating look back into Malaga's Moorish past and is an essential part of experiencing the historical depth and cultural richness of the city.

Malaga Cathedral

- **Location:** Nestled in the vibrant heart of Malaga's historic center, the cathedral dominates the city's skyline and is easily accessible from most central areas.

- **Description:** Known locally as "La Manquita," meaning "the one-armed lady," Malaga Cathedral is famed for its incomplete south tower, which gives the building its unique nickname. The cathedral is a stunning example of Renaissance and Baroque architecture, featuring a richly decorated interior with impressive columns, beautiful chapels, and an elaborate choir area.

- **History:** Construction of the cathedral began in the 16th century on the site of a former mosque, as was common in many parts of reconquered Spain. Work continued sporadically over the next three centuries but was never fully completed, giving the cathedral its distinctive asymmetrical appearance.

- **How to Get There:** You can walk to the cathedral from most parts of central Malaga. The main entrance is located just a few steps away from the bustling Calle Larios, the main shopping street.

- **Fares:** The entrance fee is about €6.00 for adults. This includes access to the cathedral, its museum, and sometimes the roof, providing a panoramic view of the city (check availability for roof tours when you visit).

- **How to Explore:** You're welcome to explore the cathedral on your own, or you can opt for an audio guide that offers detailed explanations of its history and architecture. Guided tours are also available and can enhance your understanding of this historic site.

- Opening and Closing Hours: The cathedral is open from 10:00 AM to 6:00 PM from Monday to Saturday. It is closed to tourists during mass services and special religious events.

- Tips for Visitors:

    - Check the cathedral's schedule upon arrival, as access might be restricted during religious services.

    - Be sure to dress respectfully, as this is a place of worship.

    - If the roof tour is available, don't miss it. The climb is worth the effort for the breathtaking views over Malaga.

    - Allow yourself about 1 hour to fully appreciate the architecture, art, and serene atmosphere inside the cathedral.

Visiting Malaga Cathedral offers you a profound glimpse into the city's spiritual heart and architectural grandeur. It's a must-see for anyone interested in the rich tapestry of history and culture that shapes Malaga.

Roman Theatre

- Location: The Roman Theatre is conveniently situated right at the foot of the Alcazaba fortress, in the historical center of Malaga, making it a perfect starting point for a tour through the city's ancient sites.

- Description: This ancient structure is Malaga's oldest monument, dating back to the 1st century BC. Discovered in 1951 during city landscaping, the theatre has since been carefully restored. It showcases the classical Roman architectural style with semicircular seating tiers that once accommodated spectators who gathered to watch theatrical performances.

- History: The theatre was actively used for around 300 years before being repurposed in the Middle Ages, providing materials for the construction of the Alcazaba and other buildings. Its excavation and restoration have offered valuable insights into Roman urban life and culture in Malaga.

- How to Get There: Access to the Roman Theatre is straightforward given its central location. It is within walking distance from the main tourist areas and is directly adjacent to the Alcazaba, making it easy to combine visits to both attractions.

- Fares: Entry to the Roman Theatre is free, making it an excellent option for visitors looking to explore Malaga's history without spending extra.

- How to Explore: While the site itself can be explored on your own, there are informative display boards around the theatre that provide historical context and explain its architectural significance. For a more comprehensive understanding, consider joining one of the guided tours available that often include the Alcazaba as well.

- Opening and Closing Hours: The theatre is open to visitors from 10:00 AM to 6:00 PM in winter, and until 9:00 PM in summer. These hours can vary, so it's a good idea to check ahead of your visit.

- Tips for Visitors:

    - Since the theatre is an open-air monument, it's wise to check the weather forecast and plan your visit accordingly.

    - The seating area offers little shade, so bring a hat and sunscreen if you visit during a sunny day.

    - As the seating steps can be uneven and steep, wear comfortable shoes for your safety and comfort.

    - Photography is allowed, so bring your camera to capture the historical ambiance of this remarkable site.

Exploring the Roman Theatre not only provides a peek into Malaga's Roman past but also offers a unique backdrop that contrasts with the bustling modern city. It's an essential experience for those interested in archaeology and ancient history.

Museums and Art

Picasso Museum

- Location: Nestled in the historic Buenavista Palace in the heart of Malaga, the Picasso Museum is easily accessible and close to other major attractions in the city center.

- Description: Dedicated to the city's most famous son, Pablo Picasso, the museum houses an extensive collection of his works. The exhibitions span his entire career, showcasing over 200 pieces including paintings, drawings, sculptures, and ceramics.

- History: The museum was established in response to Picasso's own desire for his work to be present in the city of his birth. Opened in 2003, the museum was a collaborative effort between the Andalusian government and the Picasso family, particularly Christine and Bernard Ruiz-Picasso, who donated many of the works.

- How to Get There: Located in the historic center of Malaga, the museum is within walking distance from most parts of the city. It's particularly close to the Malaga Cathedral and the Roman Theatre, making it a convenient addition to any sightseeing itinerary.

- Fares: Entry costs approximately €9 for adults with concessions available for students, seniors, and children. Free entry is offered on Sundays during the last two hours before closing.

- How to Explore: You can explore the museum at your own pace, appreciating Picasso's artworks and learning about his contributions to modern art. Audio guides are available in multiple languages, offering deeper insights into specific pieces and the stages of his artistic evolution.

- Opening and Closing Hours: The museum is open from 10:00 AM to 7:00 PM from November to February, and from 10:00 AM to 8:00 PM from March to October.

- Tips for Visitors:
    - Consider visiting during the free entry period on Sundays for a more budget-friendly option.
    - Photography is not allowed inside the exhibition rooms, but you can take photos in the courtyard and the museum entrance.
    - Check the museum's website for temporary exhibitions and special events that may be of interest.
    - The museum also offers workshops and educational programs that are especially appealing if you're traveling with children.

Visiting the Picasso Museum not only provides an insight into the diverse and prolific creativity of Picasso but also reflects the deep cultural heritage of Malaga, making it a must-visit for art lovers and history enthusiasts alike.

Centre Pompidou Malaga

- Location: Situated at the vibrant Muelle Uno, part of Malaga's revamped port area, the Centre Pompidou Malaga brings a slice of French culture to the Costa del Sol. It's easily recognizable by its colorful glass cube entrance, a local landmark.

- **Description:** As the first branch of the famous Parisian Centre Pompidou to be opened outside of France, this museum offers a unique cultural experience through its diverse collection of modern and contemporary art. The exhibits range from paintings and sculptures to installations and video art, featuring works by both renowned international artists and emerging talents.

- **History:** Opened in 2015, the Centre Pompidou Malaga represents a partnership between the French museum and the city of Malaga, aimed at enhancing the cultural exchange and enriching the local art scene. This initiative is part of a broader effort to transform Malaga into a world-class destination for art lovers.

- **How to Get There:** The museum is accessible on foot from downtown Malaga or via public transport. Being in the popular port area, it is close to other attractions and dining options, making it a convenient stop during a day of sightseeing.

- **Fares:** Entry costs approximately €9 for adults, with reduced rates available for students, seniors, and large groups. Free access is available every Sunday during the last two hours before the museum closes.

- **How to Explore:** You can explore the museum independently or opt for a guided tour to gain deeper insights into the artworks and the museum's vision. Audio guides are also available for a more self-paced, informative visit.

- Opening and Closing Hours: The museum is open from 9:30 AM to 8:00 PM daily, except Tuesdays when it's closed.

- Tips for Visitors:
    - Check the museum's official website before your visit to learn about any special exhibitions or events taking place.
    - Allocate at least a couple of hours to fully appreciate the diverse art collections and interactive displays.
    - The area around the museum, with its shops, restaurants, and scenic views of the port, is perfect for a leisurely stroll or a relaxing meal after your museum visit.
    - Remember that the museum's shop offers unique art-related gifts and books, ideal for souvenirs or gifts.

The Centre Pompidou Malaga is a cultural beacon for those intrigued by modern artistic expressions and seeking a contemporary complement to the historical and traditional offerings of Malaga.

Carmen Thyssen Museum

- Location: Located in the beautiful 16th-century Palacio de Villalón, in the heart of Malaga's historic district, the Carmen Thyssen Museum is easily accessible and close to other major attractions such as the Malaga Cathedral and the Picasso Museum.

- Description: The museum specializes in 19th-century Spanish painting, primarily focusing on Andalusian art. It boasts an impressive collection of works by Spanish masters, offering visitors a deep dive into the romantic and picturesque scenes of old Spain. The collection, derived from the personal collection of Baroness Carmen Thyssen-Bornemisza, includes significant works depicting traditional Spanish festivals, landscapes, and cultural practices.

- History: Opened in 2011, the museum was established to house and display Baroness Thyssen's extensive private collection, with a particular emphasis on Spanish and Andalusian art. It serves not only as a museum but also as a cultural center, contributing significantly to the artistic and cultural landscape of Malaga.

- How to Get There: Nestled in the bustling streets of Malaga's old town, the museum is just a short walk from major public transport stops and is well-signposted throughout the city.

- Fares: General admission is approximately €10, with reduced prices for students, seniors, and groups. The museum offers free entry every Sunday during the last two hours before closing.

- How to Explore: Visitors can explore the museum independently or join one of the guided tours available for a more structured experience. Audio guides are available in multiple languages, offering detailed commentary on the key artworks and themes of the collection.

- Opening and Closing Hours: The museum operates from 10:00 AM to 8:00 PM, Tuesday through Sunday. It is closed on Mondays, except on public holidays.

- Tips for Visitors:

- Plan to visit on a Sunday afternoon to take advantage of the free entry period.

- Allow plenty of time to explore not only the permanent collection but also any temporary exhibitions that might be on.

- The museum's café offers a charming spot for a coffee or snack in a setting surrounded by art, perfect for a break during your visit.

- The museum shop features a variety of art-related merchandise, books, and unique gifts, ideal for picking up souvenirs of your visit.

The Carmen Thyssen Museum is a must-visit for art lovers and those interested in exploring the rich cultural heritage of Spain through its art. It provides a perfect blend of educational and visual enjoyment, set within the historic charm of Malaga.

Parks and Recreation

Malaga Park (Parque de Malaga)

- Location: Stretching along the downtown area of Malaga, right between the bustling city center and the picturesque port, Malaga Park is an easily accessible oasis in the heart of the city.

- Description: Officially known as Parque de Málaga, but often simply referred to as 'El Parque,' this expansive public park is a beautifully landscaped garden that features a wide variety of tropical and subtropical flora. Its scenic walkways are lined with towering palm trees, exotic plants, and vibrant flower beds, creating a tranquil escape from the urban surroundings.

- History: Established in the late 19th century, Malaga Park was built on reclaimed land from the port. Over the years, it has been a central part of the city's landscape, providing a green haven for residents and visitors alike. The park is not only a place for leisure and relaxation but also serves as a cultural space, hosting various events and exhibitions throughout the year.

- How to Get There: Malaga Park is centrally located and easily reachable on foot from most parts of the city center. It's also well-connected by public transport, with bus stops nearby and just a short walk from the city's main metro station.

- Fares: There is no entry fee to visit Malaga Park, making it a fantastic free activity for travelers on any budget.

- How to Explore: You can stroll leisurely along the paved pathways, relax on one of the many benches, or enjoy a picnic under the shade of its lush trees. The park also features several fountains and statues that enhance its decorative appeal. For children, there are dedicated play areas where they can safely play and enjoy.

- Opening and Closing Hours: The park is open 24 hours a day, though it's best visited during daylight hours to fully appreciate its beauty and vibrant atmosphere.

- Tips for Visitors:

    - Check the local listings for any special events or temporary exhibitions that might be taking place in the park during your visit.

    - Bring sunscreen and water, especially if you plan to visit during the hot midday hours, as some areas can get quite sunny.

    - The park is ideal for photographers and nature lovers, thanks to its wide variety of plants and picturesque settings.

Malaga Park not only offers a peaceful retreat from the urban energy of Malaga but also serves as a splendid example of landscape architecture and horticultural diversity, perfect for a relaxing day out or a leisurely evening stroll.

Montes de Malaga Natural Park

- Location: Situated just a few kilometers north of Malaga city center, Montes de Malaga Natural Park is easily accessible for a quick escape into nature. This sprawling park covers thousands of hectares, offering a lush, green respite from the urban environment.

- Description: Known for its rolling hills, dense forests, and diverse wildlife, Montes de Malaga Natural Park is a paradise for nature lovers, hikers, and outdoor enthusiasts. The park features numerous trails that vary in difficulty, providing options for casual walkers as well as more avid hikers. The landscape is predominantly forested with pine and eucalyptus trees, interspersed with streams and occasionally opening up to stunning vistas of the Malaga coastline.

- History: The park was established to protect the area's natural environment, which had suffered from deforestation and erosion over the years. Today, it serves not only as a conservation area but also as a recreational space that promotes environmental education and sustainable tourism.

- How to Get There: The easiest way to reach Montes de Malaga Natural Park is by car, with a drive taking roughly 20 minutes from the city center. Public transport options include buses that run from Malaga to the park, dropping visitors at various points along the main road.

- Fares: There is no entry fee to visit Montes de Malaga Natural Park, making it an excellent option for budget-conscious travelers.

- How to Explore: You can explore the park by following one of the many marked trails. Maps and trail guides are available at the park's visitor center, where you can also learn about the park's flora and fauna. Guided tours are offered, providing insights into the natural and cultural history of the area.

- Opening and Closing Hours: The park is open year-round, 24 hours a day, although certain areas, especially the visitor center and specific recreational zones, have their own operating hours, usually from sunrise to sunset.

- Tips for Visitors:

    - Wear comfortable hiking shoes and bring water, especially during the summer months when temperatures can be quite high.

    - Consider packing a picnic, as there are several scenic spots throughout the park perfect for a relaxing break.

    - Keep an eye out for local wildlife, including birds of prey, which are often seen soaring above the hills.

    - Check weather conditions before heading out, as trails can be slippery after rain and fog can reduce visibility.

Visiting Montes de Malaga Natural Park offers a refreshing counterpoint to the bustling cityscape of Malaga, providing ample opportunities for physical activity, relaxation, and connection with nature. Whether you're looking for a vigorous hike or a peaceful walk, this natural park is a must-visit destination for anyone wanting to experience the natural beauty of the region.

ENTERTAINMENT AND NIGHTLIFE

Flamenco Shows

- Experience: For a truly captivating and authentic Spanish experience, attending a flamenco show in Malaga is a must. Flamenco is not just a dance; it's a profound cultural expression, combining passionate dance, soulful singing, and rhythmic guitar playing that tells stories of life, struggle, and celebration. Malaga, being in the heart of Andalusia, offers some of the most vibrant and emotional flamenco performances.

- Locations: Flamenco shows are held in various venues around the city, from intimate tablao (flamenco venues) settings to larger theatres. Popular spots include the historic Tablao Los Amayas in the picturesque La Malagueta neighborhood, and Kelipé Centro de Arte Flamenco, known for its intense and intimate performances.

- How to Get There: Most flamenco venues are centrally located and easily accessible by foot from main tourist areas or by public transport. Taxis are also a convenient option for reaching these venues.

- Ticket Prices: Prices can vary depending on the venue and the type of show. They typically range from €20 to €50, often including a drink or a full dinner with the performance.

- Best Time to Visit: Flamenco shows usually take place in the evenings, starting around 9:00 PM, making them a perfect after-dinner activity. It's wise to check schedules and book in advance as shows can fill up quickly, especially during the tourist season.

- Tips for Visitors:

    - Opt for venues that offer authentic experiences rather than tourist traps. Look for tablaos or cultural centers dedicated to flamenco.

    - Arrive early to secure good seating, as many venues operate on a first-come, first-served basis, especially those that are smaller and more intimate.

    - Listen to the different components of the performance—the guitar, singing, and dancing—to fully appreciate the complexity and emotional depth of flamenco.

    - Consider attending a show that includes an interactive segment or a mini-lesson before the performance to deepen your understanding and appreciation of the art form.

Flamenco shows in Malaga provide an unforgettable night out, filled with emotional intensity and cultural richness that is both entertaining and enlightening. Whether you are a flamenco aficionado or new to the art, these performances are sure to leave a lasting impression.

Nightclubs and Bars

- Overview: Malaga, a vibrant city with a lively nightlife scene, boasts a diverse array of nightclubs and bars that cater to all tastes. From chic rooftop bars offering panoramic views of the city to bustling nightclubs where you can dance until dawn, there's something for everyone in Malaga's nightlife.

- Popular Venues:

    - Sala Gold: This is one of Malaga's most popular nightclubs, known for its glamorous ambiance and exciting DJ sets that keep the dance floor lively with the latest hits in pop, electronic, and hip hop music.

    - The Clarence Jazz Club: For a more relaxed evening, this venue offers live jazz music in a cozy, sophisticated setting. It's a great spot to enjoy some of the finest local and international jazz acts.

    - Terraza Larios: This rooftop bar is perfect for those who appreciate a good cocktail accompanied by stunning views of Malaga's historic center and the Mediterranean Sea.

- How to Get There: Most of Malaga's top nightclubs and bars are located in the city center, easily accessible on foot from main tourist areas. Public transport, such as buses and taxis, are also readily available for those staying further afield.

- Entry Fees and Prices: Entry fees for nightclubs typically range from €10 to €20, which might include one drink. Bars usually do not have an entry fee, and drinks prices vary widely depending on the type of bar and its location. Expect to pay anywhere from €3 for a beer in a casual bar to €12 or more for a cocktail in a high-end rooftop bar.

- Best Time to Visit: Nightlife in Malaga starts late, with many bars not filling up until after 10:00 PM and nightclubs getting busy around midnight. The peak hours are from midnight to around 3:00 AM. On weekends, many venues stay open until 6:00 AM or later.

- Tips for Visitors:

    - Dress code can vary by venue; nightclubs tend to have a stricter dress code than bars. It's advisable to check in advance and dress accordingly.

    - Always have your ID handy, as most clubs and bars will check it before allowing entry, especially if you look under 25.

    - Consider starting your night at a tapas bar or a casual pub to experience the local bar culture before heading to a nightclub.

    - Take advantage of any promotional nights or happy hours to enjoy drinks at a reduced price.

    - If planning to visit multiple venues in one night, inquire about any pub crawl tours which can be a fun and safe way to explore Malaga's nightlife scene and meet new people.

Malaga's nightclubs and bars offer a vibrant mix of environments and experiences that can cater to every mood, from laid-back evenings of jazz and cocktails to energetic nights of dancing and music. Whether you're looking to mingle with locals, enjoy live music, or just soak up the lively atmosphere, Malaga's nightlife won't disappoint.

Family-Friendly Activities

- Overview: Malaga isn't just for nightlife enthusiasts; it offers a plethora of family-friendly activities that allow all ages to enjoy the vibrant culture and beautiful scenery. Whether it's interactive museums, tranquil parks, or adventurous excursions, Malaga has something to keep every member of the family entertained.

- Popular Activities:

    - Interactive Science Museum (Museo Principia): An engaging science center where children can explore various exhibits that make learning fun and interactive. The museum features hands-on displays covering topics from physics to biology, ideal for sparking curiosity in young minds.

    - Malaga Park (Parque de Málaga): This lush park offers a great escape with plenty of space for children to run and play. There are several playgrounds and a bandstand where live music performances are often held, providing entertainment for the whole family.

    - Bioparc Fuengirola: Just a short train ride from Malaga, this immersive zoo specializes in tropical forests and sustainable habitats. Unlike traditional zoos, animals live together in recreated ecosystems, which makes for an educational and unique wildlife experience.

    - Aqualand Torremolinos: A hit during the warmer months, this water park offers a variety of water slides, pools, and splash areas that are perfect for cooling off and having fun.

- How to Get There: Most family-friendly attractions are accessible via public transport, such as buses and trains. Those within Malaga city are easily reachable on foot or by a short taxi ride.

- Entry Fees and Prices: Prices vary by attraction. Museo Principia offers affordable entry fees around €3-€5, while admission to Bioparc Fuengirola is approximately €20 for adults and €15 for children. Aqualand has varied pricing, often around €25-€30 for a day pass, with discounts available if booked in advance online.

- Best Time to Visit: Early morning or late afternoon visits can help avoid crowds and the midday heat, especially during the summer. Weekdays are generally less crowded than weekends.

- Tips for Visitors:

    - Check for family tickets or group discounts which can make these outings more economical.

    - Many outdoor activities are season-dependent, especially water parks and some outdoor adventures, so check operational months and hours before planning your visit.

    - Packing sunscreen, hats, and water is essential when planning outdoor activities in Malaga, particularly in the summer months.

    - Consider timing your visits to museums during special workshops or events tailored for children for an enhanced experience.

    - Always have a plan for meals or snacks, as exploring can build up an appetite, especially in kids. Look for family-friendly restaurants or pack a picnic when visiting parks or outdoor attractions.

Malaga offers a treasure trove of activities that cater to families, ensuring that even the youngest travelers can enjoy their visit to this vibrant city. From educational museum trips to exciting days out in nature, there's no shortage of options to create memorable family moments.

Live Music Venues

- Overview: Malaga's live music scene is as vibrant and diverse as the city itself, featuring an array of venues that host everything from local flamenco artists to international rock bands. Whether you're in the mood for jazz, rock, pop, or traditional Spanish music, Malaga offers a dynamic setting to experience live performances.

- Popular Venues:

    - La Casa Invisible: A cultural hotspot located in the heart of the city, this venue is part community center, part concert hall. It regularly hosts live music nights featuring a variety of genres, making it a favorite among locals and tourists alike.

    - Clarence Jazz Club: Known for its intimate atmosphere, this venue offers a sophisticated night out with some of the best jazz performances in the city. Located in the historic center, it's the perfect spot to enjoy live music along with a glass of fine wine or a classic cocktail.

    - Sala Paris 15: As one of Malaga's largest concert halls, Sala Paris 15 attracts international acts across various music genres. From rock concerts to electronic dance music events, this venue is all about high-energy performances.

- Theatro Club Málaga: A unique venue that combines theatrical performances with live music. Located in a refurbished theater, it offers a quirky and eclectic environment where you can catch everything from indie bands to DJ nights.

- How to Get There: Most live music venues are centrally located and easily accessible on foot from many areas of Malaga. Public transportation options like buses and taxis are also available for venues that are a bit further out.

- Entry Fees and Prices: Entry fees can vary significantly depending on the artist and venue. Small bars or cafes might host free live music nights with the expectation that you buy a drink or two, whereas tickets for larger concerts in venues like Sala Paris 15 can range from €15 to over €50 for well-known artists.

- Best Time to Visit: Live music is typically an evening event, starting around 9 PM or later. Weekends are particularly popular for catching live performances, though some venues offer mid-week shows which can be less crowded.

- Tips for Visitors:
    - Check the event schedule in advance and consider purchasing tickets online to avoid missing out on popular shows.
    - Arrive early to secure good seating or a good spot near the stage, especially in smaller venues.

- Be mindful of the cultural nuances; some genres like flamenco are deeply rooted in local traditions and the audience is expected to respect the performers by being attentive and applauding at appropriate moments.

- Explore local listings or ask at your accommodation for recommendations on where to catch the best live music during your stay.

Malaga's live music venues provide an excellent backdrop to experience the city's cultural diversity and vibrant nightlife. Whether you're looking to enjoy a relaxed evening of jazz or a lively rock concert, there's always something musical happening in Malaga.

SHOPPING

Local Markets

- Overview: Shopping in Malaga's local markets is not just about buying; it's an immersive experience that lets you savor the local lifestyle, taste authentic food, and discover unique artisan products. These markets are vibrant hubs of activity where locals and tourists alike come to shop for fresh produce, handmade goods, and eclectic items.

- Popular Markets:

    - Atarazanas Market: Housed in a beautifully restored 19th-century iron building, this central market is the heartbeat of Malaga's culinary scene. Here, you can find everything from fresh fish and meats to exotic fruits and spices. The architecture alone, with its stunning stained glass, is worth the visit.

    - Mercado de la Merced: Located close to the birthplace of Picasso, this market is smaller but vibrant, offering a mix of fresh produce and local crafts. It's also a great spot to try some local tapas from one of the many food stalls.

    - El Zoco de Muelle Uno: Situated by the port, this outdoor market operates mainly on Sundays and is perfect for those looking for arts, crafts, and second-hand goods. It's an excellent place for finding unique gifts and enjoying the sea views.

- Calle San Juan: This is not a traditional market but a shopping street known for its small, independent shops selling everything from local ceramics and textiles to gourmet foods and fine wines.

- How to Get There: The Atarazanas Market is located in the city center, easily accessible on foot from most parts of central Malaga or via bus. Mercado de la Merced is also centrally located, just a short walk from Plaza de la Merced. El Zoco de Muelle Uno is best reached by walking along the Malaga port, while Calle San Juan is in the heart of the historic district.

- Shopping Hours: Local markets typically open early in the morning around 8:00 AM and close in the early afternoon, around 2:00 PM to 3:00 PM. Some food stalls might open longer, especially in tourist areas. Sunday markets like El Zoco de Muelle Uno are exceptions, usually operating from the morning until early evening.

- Tips for Visitors:

    - Bring cash, as many vendors do not accept credit cards, especially in smaller markets.

    - Go early to get the freshest produce and avoid the crowds that accumulate later in the day.

    - Don't hesitate to sample or ask questions about the products; vendors are typically proud of their goods and happy to share their knowledge.

    - Haggling is not common in food markets but can be acceptable at craft or flea markets if done respectfully.

- Take the opportunity to try some local delicacies at the market; it's a great way to dive into the local cuisine.

Malaga's local markets offer a delightful array of sights, sounds, and smells. They are ideal places to explore the rich culinary landscape of the region, hunt for handmade treasures, and experience the daily life of Malaguenos. Whether you're a food lover or a souvenir hunter, these markets promise a colorful and memorable shopping experience.

Shopping Centers

- Overview: If you're looking to combine comfort, variety, and convenience while shopping in Malaga, the city's modern shopping centers are your go-to destinations. Offering a wide range of international and Spanish brands, these centers also feature entertainment options, dining venues, and sometimes even cultural events, making them perfect for a full-day outing.

- Popular Shopping Centers:

    - Centro Comercial Larios Centro: Located near the city center, Larios Centro is one of Malaga's most popular shopping malls. It hosts over 100 stores including international favorites like Zara, H&M, and Mango, alongside a variety of local shops. The mall also features a multiplex cinema and numerous eateries.

    - Centro Comercial Vialia Malaga: This shopping center is conveniently located within the Maria Zambrano train station, making it easily accessible for those arriving by train. Vialia offers a wide selection of shops, from clothing to electronics, and includes a food court and a cinema.

- Malaga Plaza: Nestled in the heart of the city, Malaga Plaza is known for its relaxed shopping atmosphere. It boasts a good mix of national and international retail stores, along with cosmetic shops, tech stores, and several cafes.

- Plaza Mayor Shopping and Leisure Center: Just outside the city center, Plaza Mayor is a sprawling complex that resembles a traditional Andalusian village. It features not only a large selection of shops but also a cinema complex, bowling alley, and many restaurants. It's particularly popular among families and groups looking for a varied entertainment experience.

- How to Get There: Larios Centro and Malaga Plaza are within walking distance from most central locations in Malaga or a short bus ride. Vialia is part of the train station complex, so it's extremely accessible if you're arriving by train or bus. Plaza Mayor is best reached by car or the suburban train, with a dedicated stop at "Plaza Mayor" making it convenient for visitors.

- Shopping Hours: Most shopping centers in Malaga open around 10:00 AM and close around 10:00 PM. These hours may extend during the holiday seasons or special sale periods.

- Tips for Visitors:

- Look out for seasonal sales, especially during the summer and after Christmas, when discounts can be very significant.

- If you're driving to Plaza Mayor or any large shopping center, remember to note where you parked as parking areas can be vast.

- Check the shopping center's event calendar online before you visit, as many host special events, workshops, or live shows that you might want to join.

- Make use of the locker facilities available in larger centers to store your purchases as you continue shopping or enjoy other leisure activities within the complex.

Shopping centers in Malaga offer more than just shopping; they provide a complete entertainment experience that can include movies, meals, and even occasional cultural events. Whether you're looking for the latest fashion trends, tech gadgets, or just a pleasant day out, these centers cover all bases.

Boutique Shops

- Overview: For those who cherish unique styles and personalized shopping experiences, Malaga's boutique shops offer a delightful alternative to the mainstream retail outlets. These charming boutiques, often nestled in the historic streets of the city, provide a treasure trove of exclusive clothing, handmade accessories, and one-of-a-kind gifts, crafted by local and international designers.

- Popular Boutique Shops:

- La Temporal: Situated in the artsy Soho district, La Temporal is renowned for its eclectic mix of contemporary fashion and traditional craftsmanship. This boutique is a must-visit for fashion enthusiasts looking for something different from the usual high street offerings.

- Epoca: A boutique that specializes in vintage and retro clothing, Epoca offers a carefully curated selection of garments from the 20th century. It's a fantastic spot for fashion lovers and collectors seeking high-quality vintage dresses, bags, and jewelry.

- Boutique Paloma: Located in the picturesque Old Town, Boutique Paloma showcases a range of women's clothing focusing on chic, Mediterranean-inspired styles. It's perfect for finding elegant outfits for both casual and formal occasions.

- El Caleidoscopio: This vibrant shop features handcrafted jewelry, art, and decorative items made by local artists. It's a colorful place to discover unique gifts and souvenirs that embody the spirit of Malaga.

- How to Get There: Most boutique shops in Malaga are located in the city center, particularly around the historic district and Soho area. These locations are easily accessible on foot from many parts of the city or by using local buses.

- Shopping Hours: Boutique shops typically open around 10:00 AM and close around 8:00 PM. However, hours can vary, especially in the Old Town, where shops might close for a traditional siesta in the afternoon.

- Tips for Visitors:

    - Take your time to explore the smaller streets and alleyways of Malaga's Old Town and Soho district where many boutiques are hidden. It's not just about shopping but also enjoying the architectural and cultural ambiance.

    - Many boutique shops are owned and run by the designers themselves. Engage with them to learn more about the inspiration behind their collections and the stories of their crafts.

    - Check if there are any local fashion or shopping events during your visit, as boutiques often participate with special promotions or limited-edition items.

    - Since many boutiques offer unique pieces, they might not always have a wide range of sizes. If you find something you love but it doesn't fit, ask if there is a possibility for adjustments or similar designs in your size.

Shopping in Malaga's boutique shops is not merely about acquiring new items; it's an intimate experience that connects you with the local culture and creativity. These small, often family-run stores not only provide exclusive products but also represent the heart and soul of Malaga's artistic community.

Souvenir Recommendations

- Overview: No visit to Malaga is complete without bringing back a few souvenirs that capture the essence of this vibrant Andalusian city. From local crafts to gastronomic delights,

Malaga offers a wide array of memorabilia that make perfect gifts for your loved ones or keepsakes for yourself.

- Popular Souvenir Choices:
    - Local Crafts: Hand-painted ceramics and tiles reflecting Malaga's Moorish and Roman heritage are beautiful and functional keepsakes. You can find these in many boutiques in the Old Town or at artisan markets. Look for pieces that feature traditional Andalusian patterns.
    - Food and Wine: Olive oil is a staple of Spanish cuisine and some of the best in the world comes from the Andalusia region. Purchase from local markets or specialty shops where you can often taste before you buy. Malaga is also famous for its sweet fortified wine, Moscatel, which makes a great gift for wine enthusiasts.
    - Fashion and Accessories: Esparto grass products, including shoes, bags, and mats, are traditional in Malaga and reflect the rustic charm of the area. These items are not only stylish but also incredibly durable.
    - Art and Literature: Consider buying prints or small paintings from local artists, which depict the beautiful landscapes and urban scenes of Malaga. Additionally, books about or from local Andalusian authors can be a wonderful souvenir for the literary minded.
- Where to Shop:

- Atarazanas Market and Mercado de la Merced are great for edible souvenirs like spices, almonds, and olives.

- Calle Larios and surrounding streets have various shops offering regional crafts and modern Spanish fashion.

- Soho District provides opportunities to buy original art directly from local artists' galleries and studios.

- Shopping Tips:

    - When purchasing food items, make sure they meet the import regulations of your home country to avoid any inconvenience at customs.

    - For ceramics and other fragile items, ask the seller to pack them securely, or consider carrying them in your hand luggage.

    - Haggle with vendors, especially in markets or street stalls—it is often expected and can help you get a better deal.

    - Keep receipts of higher-value purchases, as you might be eligible for tax refunds at the airport before leaving Spain.

Bringing home souvenirs from Malaga allows you to preserve the memories of your journey in a tangible form. Whether it's a bottle of local wine to share with friends or a handmade ceramic piece for your home, each item has a story worth telling.

FESTIVALS AND EVENTS

Malaga Carnival

- Overview: The Malaga Carnival is an explosion of color, music, and exuberance, taking place annually in the lead-up to Lent. This vibrant festival showcases the rich cultural tapestry of Malaga through elaborate parades, flamboyant costumes, and spirited performances, making it a must-experience event for visitors.

- Location: The festivities are scattered throughout the city, with major events held in historic city center areas like Plaza de la Constitución and Calle Larios.

- What to Expect:

    - Parades: The heart of the Carnival is its grand parades, featuring dazzling floats, intricate costumes, and throngs of dancers moving to the rhythms of samba and flamenco beats. The Grand Parade is the highlight, usually occurring on the weekend before Ash Wednesday.

    - Costume Contests: Both locals and visitors dress up in creative and often humorous costumes. Participating in or watching the costume contests can be a highlight of the Carnival.

    - Singing Competitions: Attend the traditional 'murga' and 'comparsa' competitions, where groups perform satirical and humorous songs that comment on current events and social issues.

- Children's Events: Family-friendly activities, including children's parades and costume contests, ensure that there's plenty of fun for younger visitors as well.

- Dates: The dates vary each year but typically occur in February or early March. It's advisable to check the exact dates when planning your visit.

- Tips for Visitors:

    - Arrive early to secure a good viewing spot for parades and performances, as the streets can get very crowded.

    - Dress up! Joining in with a costume can enhance your experience and help you feel a part of the festivities.

    - Use public transport to get to the carnival events, as parking can be challenging during the festival.

    - Keep valuables secure and be mindful of your belongings in crowded areas.

- Other Information:

    - After the main events, don't miss the 'Burial of the Sardine' (Entierro del Boquerón), which marks the end of the Carnival. This quirky tradition involves a mock funeral procession that symbolizes the burial of the past, allowing the community to prepare for Lent with a clean slate.

The Malaga Carnival offers a unique glimpse into the local traditions and communal spirit of the city. Engaging in this lively celebration will not only provide entertainment but also deepen your appreciation for Andalusian culture.

Holy Week (Semana Santa)

- Overview: Holy Week in Malaga, known as Semana Santa, is one of the most profound and spectacular religious events in Spain, drawing visitors from around the globe. This week-long celebration leading up to Easter is filled with solemn processions, artistic pasos (floats), and deeply rooted religious traditions.

- Location: Processions wind through various parts of Malaga, but the most spectacular routes are typically along the main thoroughfares such as Calle Larios and the historic city center.

- What to Expect:

    - Processions: Different brotherhoods (cofradías) carry elaborate pasos depicting scenes from the Passion of Christ. These are often ornately decorated and carried by costaleros (bearers) amidst clouds of incense and the glow of candles.

    - Marching Bands: Each procession is accompanied by marching bands playing traditional Semana Santa music, which adds a solemn and emotional backdrop to the events.

    - Crowds: The city swells with visitors and locals alike, all eager to participate in or observe the processions. The atmosphere, though crowded, is charged with devotion and passion.

- Dates: Holy Week dates change annually depending on the Christian calendar, typically occurring in March or April.

- Tips for Visitors:

- Plan your visit well in advance, as accommodations can be hard to find close to the event dates.

- Wear comfortable shoes and be prepared for a lot of standing or walking, as processions can last several hours.

- Pick a spot early if you want to watch the processions from a particular location, as prime viewing areas can get crowded quickly.

- Be respectful of the solemnity and religious significance of the processions, especially if you are taking photos.

- Other Information:

  - Night Processions: Some of the most emotional moments occur during the night processions, where the solemnity and the play of light and shadows create an unforgettable atmosphere.

  - Children's Participation: It's common to see children dressed in traditional robes participating in the processions or handing out traditional Easter sweets to the crowd.

  - Security: Given the size of the crowds, security is tight, but the events are generally very safe. Following local guidance and respecting barriers set up for crowd control will ensure a good experience.

Holy Week in Malaga is not just a tourist attraction; it's a cultural and spiritual experience that offers deep insight into the Andalusian soul. The combination of art, music, and communal participation makes it a profoundly moving event that resonates long after the festivities have concluded.

Malaga Fair (Feria de Málaga)

- Overview: The Malaga Fair is one of the biggest and most vibrant celebrations in Spain, marking the re-conquest of the city by the Catholic Monarchs in 1487. This week-long festival is a wonderful blend of traditional and modern festivities, featuring live music, dancing, traditional foods, and fireworks, making it a thrilling cultural experience for both locals and tourists.

- Location: The fair is split between two main areas: the historic city center, where daytime festivities take place, and the Cortijo de Torres fairground, the hub for nighttime celebrations.

- What to Expect:

    - Daytime Festivities: The city center comes alive with traditional Andalusian music and dance, particularly flamenco, as locals don traditional costumes. The streets are filled with people, horse-drawn carriages, and impromptu performances.

    - Nighttime Celebrations: The fairground at Cortijo de Torres transforms into a lively festival with amusement rides, live concerts, dance pavilions (casetas), and a wide variety of food stalls. The atmosphere is electric, with music ranging from traditional Spanish to modern pop and rock.

- Fireworks: The opening night is marked by a spectacular fireworks display, which can be viewed from many parts of the city.

- Bullfights: During the fair, La Malagueta bullring hosts a series of bullfights, attracting some of the finest matadors from across Spain.

• Dates: Typically held in August, the exact dates can vary slightly each year.

• Tips for Visitors:

- Wear comfortable clothing and footwear as temperatures can be quite high and you might be on your feet for extended periods.

- Try the local food at the fair, especially dishes like 'espetos' (sardines skewered and cooked over a charcoal grill) and 'porra antequerana' (a cold tomato soup).

- Visit both the daytime and nighttime festivities to fully experience the contrast and full spectrum of the fair.

- Keep hydrated and apply sunscreen regularly — August in Malaga can be extremely hot.

• Other Information:

- Transportation: Public transportation is usually enhanced during the fair with increased bus and train services, especially routes to and from the fairground.

- Accommodations: It's advisable to book your accommodations well in advance as the city gets very crowded during the fair.

- Cultural Significance: Engaging with the locals and participating in the dances or simply wearing a traditional hat can enrich your experience.

The Malaga Fair offers a unique opportunity to dive into the heart of Andalusian culture, filled with joyous celebration and colorful traditions. It's a perfect time to experience the warmth and hospitality of Malaga's people, making it a highlight of any visit to the city.

Malaga Film Festival

- Overview: The Malaga Film Festival, officially known as the Festival de Málaga Cine en Español, is a prestigious event celebrating Spanish-language cinema. It offers a platform for filmmakers from the Spanish-speaking world to showcase their work, ranging from feature films to documentaries and shorts. The festival also aims to promote the development and dissemination of Spanish-language film and foster discussions among artists and audiences.

- Location: The main events are hosted at the iconic Cervantes Theatre and the Echegaray Theatre, along with other venues across Malaga, including cinemas and cultural centers.

- What to Expect:
    - Screenings: Attend a variety of film screenings that include a mix of new releases, indie films, and critically acclaimed projects. Each screening often

ends with a Q&A session where directors and cast discuss the film with the audience.

- Awards: The festival culminates in an awards ceremony, recognizing excellence in various categories such as Best Film, Best Director, Best Actor, and Best Actress.

- Workshops and Panels: Participate in workshops and panel discussions that cover various aspects of filmmaking, from production to distribution, led by industry experts.

- Networking Events: The festival serves as a networking hub for professionals in the Spanish-speaking film industry, providing numerous opportunities to meet filmmakers, actors, producers, and other industry insiders.

- Dates: The festival typically takes place in March or April, and the exact dates can vary each year.

- Tips for Visitors:

    - Plan your schedule in advance to make the most of the film screenings and events, as they can overlap.

    - Purchase tickets early, especially for high-profile screenings and talks, which can sell out quickly.

    - If you're interested in the technical side of filmmaking, look out for industry-specific sessions that can offer deep insights and learning opportunities.

- Be ready to embrace the festival atmosphere; enjoy the mix of casual street encounters and formal events.

- Other Information:

    - Language: While the primary focus is on Spanish-language films, many screenings feature subtitles, making them accessible to non-Spanish speakers.

    - Accessibility: Most venues are equipped to accommodate guests with disabilities, but it's wise to check accessibility options in advance if needed.

    - Visitor Services: Information booths and festival volunteers are usually available to help with directions, program updates, and general inquiries.

The MALAGA Film Festival not only enriches the cultural landscape of the city but also provides a vibrant forum for the celebration of Spanish-language cinema. It's an essential event for film enthusiasts eager to explore new trends and witness the evolving narratives within the Spanish-speaking filmmaking community.

OUTDOOR ACTIVITIES

Beaches of Malaga

- Overview: Malaga's coastline is renowned for its beautiful beaches, stretching from quiet coves to vibrant promenades lined with restaurants and bars. Whether you're looking for a spot to relax, engage in water sports, or simply soak up the sun, the beaches of Malaga offer something for everyone.

- Locations:

    - La Malagueta: Easily accessible from the city center, La Malagueta is Malaga's most famous urban beach, known for its dark sand and lively atmosphere. Located to the east of the port, it's surrounded by a bustling promenade filled with eateries and shops.

    - El Palo: Further east, El Palo is favored by locals for its traditional 'chiringuitos' (beach bars) that serve fresh seafood. This beach is excellent for experiencing local culture and enjoying water sports like paddleboarding and kayaking.

    - Playa de Pedregalejo: Known for its laid-back vibe and smaller crowd, Pedregalejo is a hit among younger visitors and families. The beach is lined with trendy cafes and traditional fish restaurants, making it a perfect spot for a relaxed day out.

- What to Expect:

    - Facilities: Most beaches in Malaga are well-equipped with showers, sunbeds for rent, lifeguards during the summer months, and accessible pathways for those with mobility concerns.

- Activities: Beyond sunbathing and swimming, many beaches offer facilities for volleyball, jet skiing, windsurfing, and more.

- Sunset Views: Malaga beaches are west-facing, providing spectacular sunset views that paint the sky in shades of orange and pink, ideal for evening strolls or romantic dinners by the sea.

- Tips for Visitors:

  - Arrive early to secure a good spot, especially during the summer months when the beaches can get quite crowded.

  - Always apply sunscreen and drink plenty of water to stay hydrated under the sun.

  - Keep an eye on personal belongings and use the lockers or storage facilities where available.

  - Respect local regulations regarding littering, noise levels, and beach etiquette to ensure a pleasant experience for everyone.

- Other Information:

  - Beach Bars and Restaurants: Don't miss trying local dishes at the beachfront 'chiringuitos' where you can enjoy fresh sardines cooked right on the beach on skewers over a wood fire.

- Nightlife: Some beaches, particularly La Malagueta and Pedregalejo, are close to nightclubs and bars, making them popular spots for evening entertainment.

- Safety: Beaches in Malaga adhere to strict safety standards, with lifeguard patrols and first aid stations readily available during peak seasons.

The beaches of Malaga are a highlight for many visitors, offering a blend of natural beauty, leisure activities, and cultural experiences. Whether it's a day of adventurous water sports or a tranquil afternoon by the sea, Malaga's beaches are sure to enhance your stay with unforgettable memories.

Hiking and Biking

- Overview: Beyond its stunning beaches, Malaga offers a diverse landscape perfect for hiking and biking enthusiasts. With its surrounding hills, rugged coastlines, and scenic countryside, Malaga provides a variety of trails that cater to all levels of experience, from leisurely rides along the coast to challenging mountain treks.

- Popular Trails:

  - Montes de Malaga Natural Park: Just a short drive from the city center, this natural park is a haven for hikers and bikers alike. It features a range of trails that meander through pine forests and offer stunning views over the city and the Mediterranean. The park is well-marked, making it easy to choose a route that suits your ability level.

- Caminito del Rey: For the more adventurous, this once notorious walkway has been restored for safety and is now a spectacular hiking route. The path clings to the side of a gorge, offering breathtaking views and a thrilling experience. It's a bit further from Malaga, but well worth the drive for avid hikers.

- Coastal Path (Senda Litoral de Malaga): Ideal for bikers and casual walkers, this mostly flat path runs along the coast connecting various beaches and towns. It offers easy access and beautiful sea views, perfect for a family outing or a relaxed cycling day.

- What to Expect:

    - Facilities: Trails in and around Malaga are generally well-maintained, with signage and rest areas. Bike rental shops are available in the city and some tourist spots, offering everything from basic bikes to high-end mountain bikes.

    - Guided Tours: Many local companies offer guided hiking and biking tours, which can provide insightful commentary and ensure you hit the best spots without getting lost.

    - Weather Conditions: Always check the weather before heading out, especially if you plan to tackle more demanding routes. Early morning is typically the best time to start in the warmer months to avoid the midday heat.

- Tips for Visitors:

- Wear appropriate footwear and clothing. Sturdy hiking shoes are recommended for rougher terrain.

- Carry sufficient water, sun protection, and snacks, especially during the summer months when temperatures can soar.

- Consider downloading a trail map on your phone or carry a physical map, especially in areas where mobile signals can be weak.

- Respect the natural environment by staying on marked paths and taking your rubbish with you.

- Other Information:

  - Wildlife: The region around Malaga is home to a variety of wildlife. Keep your eyes peeled for birds of prey, wild boars, and even mountain goats.

  - Cultural Sites: Some trails lead past historical sites like old mills, watchtowers, and traditional villages, offering a glimpse into the local heritage.

  - Photography Opportunities: Don't forget your camera, as these trails offer some of the most picturesque vistas in the region.

Hiking and biking in Malaga are not only great physical activities but also a chance to connect with nature and experience the breathtaking landscapes that the region has to offer. Whether you're a seasoned hiker looking for a new challenge or a family looking for a pleasant day out, Malaga's trails provide a memorable outdoor adventure.

Golf Courses

- Overview: Malaga, located in the heart of the Costa del Sol, is often referred to as the "Costa del Golf" due to its high concentration of top-quality golf courses. With over 70 courses in the region, it's a premier destination for golfers of all skill levels, boasting year-round sunny weather and beautifully designed courses that blend seamlessly into the picturesque landscape.

- Top Golf Courses:
    - Real Club de Campo de Malaga: This is one of the oldest golf courses in Southern Spain, offering a rich history and a mature, challenging layout. Located near the airport, it's easily accessible and offers views of the Mediterranean.

    - Baviera Golf: Situated closer to the eastern part of Malaga province, Baviera Golf is known for its well-maintained fairways and stunning mountain backdrop. It's suitable for all levels of golfers.

    - La Cala Resort: As one of the largest and most exclusive golf resorts in Southern Spain, La Cala features three 18-hole golf courses, each offering a different set of challenges amidst rolling hills and lush countryside.

- What to Expect:
    - Facilities: These golf courses offer high-standard facilities, including clubhouses, pro shops, driving ranges, and training areas. Many also feature

restaurants and bars where you can enjoy a meal or a drink after your round.

- Tournaments and Events: Many courses host local and international tournaments, which can be a great opportunity to watch professional play or participate in amateur competitions.

- Golf Lessons: Most clubs offer lessons with professional instructors, which can be booked in advance, whether you're a beginner looking to learn the basics or an experienced player aiming to fine-tune your skills.

- Tips for Visitors:

    - Booking in advance is highly recommended, especially during the peak season from April to October.

    - Check for dress codes, as many golf clubs have strict policies on appropriate attire.

    - Consider renting golf clubs if you're traveling without your equipment; most courses offer high-quality clubs for rent.

    - Stay hydrated and wear sunscreen, as rounds can last several hours under the sun.

- Other Information:

    - Accessibility: Many golf courses in Malaga are designed to be accessible, with carts available to rent, helping those with mobility issues or those who prefer a more leisurely experience.

- Environment: Golf courses in Malaga are often located in areas of natural beauty, surrounded by typical Mediterranean flora and fauna. They provide not just a sporting challenge but also a chance to enjoy the serene environment.

- Networking Opportunities: For business travelers, golf courses can be an excellent venue for meeting local professionals and networking in a relaxed setting.

Golfing in Malaga offers more than just a game; it's an experience that combines sport, nature, and relaxation in one of Spain's most scenic regions. Whether you're looking to improve your game, compete, or simply enjoy a day out on the green, Malaga's golf courses provide a world-class golfing experience.

Water Sports

- Overview: Malaga's extensive coastline and favorable climate make it a hotspot for water sports enthusiasts. From serene kayaking and paddleboarding to exhilarating jet skiing and windsurfing, the beaches and marinas of Malaga offer a variety of water-based activities suitable for all ages and skill levels.

- Popular Water Sports:

    - Kayaking and Paddleboarding: Explore the calm waters near Malagueta Beach or venture around the picturesque cliffs and coves along the coastline. Equipment rental and guided tours are widely available, providing a safe and enjoyable experience even for beginners.

- Jet Skiing: For a rush of adrenaline, jet skiing is a popular choice at many of Malaga's beaches. Rental stations can be found at major beaches where short briefings are given to first-timers to ensure safety.

- Windsurfing and Kitesurfing: The eastern beaches, particularly around the areas of Tarifa and the Costa del Sol, are renowned for their excellent wind conditions, making them ideal for windsurfing and kitesurfing. Schools and rental shops cater to both beginners and advanced surfers with equipment and classes.

- Diving and Snorkeling: The clear waters of the Mediterranean are perfect for diving and snorkeling. Discover vibrant marine life and explore underwater ecosystems at sites like the marine reserve around La Herradura, where guided dives and certification courses are offered.

- What to Expect:

    - Facilities: You'll find well-equipped centers offering rentals, lessons, and tours. These centers typically provide all the necessary gear and safety equipment.

    - Safety: Operators prioritize safety, with activities conducted under the supervision of certified instructors. It's important to follow all guidelines and instructions provided.

    - Group and Solo Options: Whether you want to enjoy a solitary paddle along the coast or join a group tour or class, there are plenty of options to suit your preference.

- Tips for Visitors:

    - Check the weather and sea conditions before planning water sports activities, especially for windsurfing or sailing.

    - Book in advance during peak tourist seasons to secure your spot and avoid disappointment.

    - Wear appropriate clothing and protective gear, such as wetsuits for prolonged water exposure, especially in cooler months.

    - Always listen to local advice and respect the marine environment, avoiding restricted areas and maintaining a safe distance from marine life.

- Other Information:

    - Accessibility: Many water sports providers offer lessons and equipment suited for children and those with limited mobility, ensuring everyone can participate.

    - Environmental Impact: Operators are increasingly conscious of their environmental impact, offering eco-friendly options and promoting clean-up dives and other conservation activities.

    - Community Events: Participate in local water sports events and competitions if you're visiting during the summer, which can be a thrilling way to engage with the local community and other enthusiasts.

Water sports in Malaga are not only a thrilling way to spend your day but also a chance to connect with nature and explore the stunning Mediterranean coastline from a unique perspective. Whether you're a seasoned athlete or a curious beginner, the diverse range of activities ensures there's something for everyone to enjoy in the water.

PRACTICAL INFORMATION

Weather and Best Times to Visit

- Overview: Malaga, nestled on Spain's southern coast, enjoys a Mediterranean climate characterized by hot summers, mild winters, and abundant sunshine, making it a year-round destination. However, the experience can vary significantly depending on the time of year, so choosing when to visit can enhance your enjoyment depending on your interests.

- Seasonal Overview:

    - Spring (March to May): This season is ideal for visitors looking to enjoy outdoor activities without the intense heat of summer. Temperatures are comfortable, ranging from 18°C to 25°C (64°F to 77°F). The countryside is lush and vibrant, making it a perfect time for hiking, cycling, and exploring the natural parks.

    - Summer (June to August): Summer is peak tourist season in Malaga, with temperatures often climbing above 30°C (86°F). The warm weather is perfect for beachgoers, water sports enthusiasts, and nighttime activities, as the city buzzes with festivals and events. However, be prepared for crowded attractions and higher prices.

    - Autumn (September to November): Like spring, autumn offers milder weather and fewer crowds, with temperatures gradually cooling from 28°C to 20°C (82°F to 68°F). It's an excellent time for cultural visits and wine tasting tours, as the region begins harvesting grapes.

- Winter (December to February): Winters are mild compared to much of Europe, with daytime temperatures rarely dropping below 12°C (54°F). It's a great time to enjoy Malaga's cultural offerings, like museums and historic sites, without the crowds. Occasional rain can occur, so packing a light raincoat is advisable.

- What to Expect:

  - Daylight Hours: Longer days in spring and summer allow more time for sightseeing and activities. Winter days are shorter, but still generally sunny.

  - Accommodation Rates: Seasonal fluctuations affect accommodation prices; expect peak rates in summer and during festivals. Winter usually offers the best deals.

  - Festivals and Events: Malaga hosts various events throughout the year that can be a major draw or a time to avoid depending on your preference for crowds.

- Tips for Visitors:

  - Always check the local weather forecast close to your travel date to pack appropriately.

  - If visiting in summer, book accommodations and activities well in advance, and be prepared for higher prices and more tourists.

- Visiting during shoulder seasons (spring and autumn) can offer a more relaxed experience with the benefit of pleasant weather and lower costs.

- Winter visits allow for a more "local" experience with fewer tourists, though some seasonal amenities might be limited.

- Other Information:

  - Sun Protection: Regardless of the season, the sun in Malaga can be strong. Always wear sunscreen, a hat, and sunglasses, especially if you plan to be outdoors for extended periods.

  - Hydration: Keep hydrated, particularly in summer when temperatures soar.

  - Cultural Sensitivity: When visiting religious sites or during holy weeks, dress conservatively and respect local customs.

Understanding the weather patterns and choosing the right time to visit Malaga can greatly influence the quality of your trip, helping you to enjoy all that the city and its surroundings have to offer in comfort. Whether you're there for the beaches, the cultural experiences, or the natural beauty, there's a perfect time in Malaga for everyone.

Health and Safety

- Overview: Malaga is generally a safe and welcoming destination for travelers. However, like any popular tourist area, it's important to stay informed about health and safety measures to ensure a pleasant and secure trip.

- Health Precautions:

    - Medical Facilities: Malaga is well-equipped with medical facilities, including hospitals and clinics that offer services to both locals and tourists. It's advisable to have travel health insurance in case of emergencies.

    - Pharmacies: Pharmacies are readily available throughout the city, and pharmacists often speak English. They can assist with minor ailments and provide over-the-counter medications.

    - Vaccinations: No special vaccinations are required for visitors to Spain, but it's recommended to be up-to-date on routine vaccinations such as measles, mumps, and rubella (MMR), as well as seasonal flu shots.

- Safety Tips:

    - Pickpocketing: Like many tourist destinations, pickpocketing can occur, especially in crowded places like tourist attractions, beaches, and public transport. Always keep an eye on your belongings and use anti-theft bags or money belts.

    - Scams: Be aware of common scams targeting tourists, such as overpriced taxi fares and street games. Always verify the identity of any person claiming to be an official or a service provider.

    - Travel Insurance: It's wise to have comprehensive travel insurance that covers theft, loss, accidents, and medical emergencies.

- Local Emergency Services:

- Emergency Number: Dial 112 for emergency services in Malaga, which can connect you to police, fire, and ambulance services. This number is toll-free and can be dialed from any phone.

- Police Presence: Malaga has a visible police presence, with local and national police forces active in maintaining safety. Police stations are approachable for assistance if needed.

• Natural Hazards:

- Heatwaves: During the summer months, temperatures can soar, leading to heatwaves. It's important to stay hydrated, seek shade during the hottest parts of the day, and use sunscreen to prevent sunburn.

- Water Safety: When engaging in water activities, always follow local guidelines and safety instructions. Pay attention to flags and signs at beaches that indicate swimming conditions.

• Tips for Visitors:

- Keep a copy of your passport and important documents separately from the originals when exploring the city.

- Use certified and marked taxis or trusted public transport options for travel, especially late at night.

- Stay informed about local weather forecasts, especially if planning outdoor activities or trips to the countryside.

• Other Information:

- Accessibility: Malaga is increasingly catering to travelers with disabilities, with improved accessibility in public areas, transport, and major tourist attractions.

- Cultural Awareness: Respect local customs and traditions, especially during religious or cultural festivals, to foster positive interactions with locals.

Being mindful of health and safety during your stay in Malaga will help ensure a stress-free and enjoyable experience. With these precautions in mind, you can fully immerse yourself in all the vibrant culture, beautiful landscapes, and exciting activities Malaga has to offer.

Money and Tipping

- Overview: Understanding the basics of money management and tipping customs in Malaga is essential for a smooth travel experience. Spain uses the Euro (€) as its currency, and tipping, while not compulsory as in some countries, is customary in various service industries.

- Currency Exchange:

    - Currency Used: The Euro (€) is the sole currency used in Malaga and throughout Spain.

    - Exchanging Money: You can exchange currency at the airport, banks, and dedicated currency exchange offices. However, banks typically offer the best rates. It's advisable to exchange a small amount at the airport if needed immediately and then look for better rates in the city.

- ATMs: ATMs are widely available throughout Malaga and are often the most convenient way to access cash. They accept international debit and credit cards, but be aware of possible fees from your bank and the local ATM provider.

- Credit and Debit Cards:

  - Acceptance: Major credit and debit cards (Visa, MasterCard, American Express) are widely accepted in shops, restaurants, and hotels. However, it's a good idea to have some cash for smaller cafes or shops that may not accept cards.

  - Security Tips: Always keep an eye on your card during transactions and cover the keypad when entering your PIN. Check statements regularly for any unauthorized charges.

- Tipping Etiquette:

  - Restaurants and Bars: It is customary to leave a tip of around 5-10% in restaurants if you are satisfied with the service, although a service charge may already be included in the bill (check for "servicio incluido"). In bars, tipping is less common, but rounding up the bill or leaving small change is appreciated.

  - Taxis: For taxis, it's usual to round up to the nearest euro, especially if the driver helps with luggage or provides good service.

  - Hotels: In hotels, tipping is appreciated but not obligatory. You might consider leaving €1-2 per day for housekeeping or a similar amount for porters per bag.

- Tour Guides: If taking a guided tour, a tip of €5-10 per person can be offered at the end of the tour if you found the guide informative and engaging.

- Budgeting Tips:

    - Daily Budget: Plan your daily budget considering meals, transportation, entrance fees for attractions, and incidental expenses. Prices in Malaga can vary; a meal in an inexpensive restaurant might cost around €10-15, while a three-course meal in a mid-range restaurant could be about €30-50 per person.

    - Cost-saving Tips: Save money by dining where locals dine, using public transportation, and visiting free attractions or on days when entrance fees are waived.

- Other Information:

    - Sales Tax: The prices displayed in shops include sales tax (VAT), so there are no additional taxes added at the checkout.

    - Financial Safety: Keep money in a secure place, like a money belt or a hotel safe, and only carry what you need for the day.

By familiarizing yourself with these money and tipping practices, you can navigate your financial interactions in Malaga with confidence, ensuring a pleasant and respectful experience in all your activities and interactions.

Language Tips

- Overview: While Spanish is the official language in Malaga, you will find that English is widely spoken in tourist areas, hotels, and restaurants. However, learning a few basic Spanish phrases can enhance your travel experience, showing respect for the local culture and often leading to friendlier interactions.

- Basic Spanish Phrases:

    - Greetings and Politeness:

        - Hello: Hola (OH-lah)

        - Goodbye: Adiós (ah-DYOS)

        - Please: Por favor (por fah-VOR)

        - Thank you: Gracias (GRAH-syas)

        - Yes: Sí (see)

        - No: No (noh)

    - Getting Around:

        - Where is...?: ¿Dónde está...? (DON-day es-TAH...?)

        - How much is it?: ¿Cuánto cuesta? (KWAN-toh KWEH-stah?)

        - I would like...: Quisiera... (kee-SYEH-rah...)

        - Help!: ¡Ayuda! (ah-YOO-dah!)

- Bathroom: Baño (BAH-nyo)

- Language Tips for Travelers:

  - Learning Resources: Consider using language apps like Duolingo, Babbel, or Rosetta Stone before and during your trip to pick up basic vocabulary and phrases.

  - Carry a Phrasebook: A small Spanish phrasebook or a translation app on your smartphone can be invaluable for quick reference in more complex or specific situations.

  - Practice Listening: Spanish in Spain can be spoken quite quickly. Try to listen to Spanish language media, such as radio or podcasts, to get accustomed to the speed and accent.

- Communication Etiquette:

  - Formal vs. Informal: Spanish has both formal (usted) and informal (tú) forms of address. Use "usted" in formal settings or with individuals who are older or in authority to show respect.

  - Non-verbal Communication: Spaniards are typically expressive and use gestures frequently. A handshake is common when meeting someone, while friends may greet with a light kiss on each cheek.

  - Speaking English: When approaching someone, it's polite to ask if they speak English before proceeding. Use the phrase, "¿Habla inglés?" (AH-blah een-GLAYS?) to inquire.

- Cultural Insights:

    - Regional Languages: Note that in some parts of Spain, other languages like Catalan, Basque, and Galician are also official alongside Spanish. However, in Malaga, Spanish is predominantly spoken.

    - Signage: Most signs and menus are in Spanish, though many tourist spots provide English translations. Learning to recognize basic words for foods and directions can be very helpful.

- Using English:

    - Tourism and Business: In tourism-heavy and business areas, English is commonly spoken, so you can typically communicate with ease in hotels, major restaurants, and at main attractions.

By integrating these language tips into your travel preparation and practice, you can navigate Malaga more smoothly and connect more meaningfully with local residents. Even a small effort in speaking the local language is often appreciated and can make your experience in this vibrant Spanish city even more enjoyable.

ITINERARIES

1 Day in Malaga

If you only have one day to explore Malaga, this itinerary ensures you experience the best of its culture, history, and ambiance. From dawn to dusk, follow this guide to make the most of your time in this vibrant city.

- Morning:

  - Start with Breakfast at a Local Café: Begin your day with a traditional Spanish breakfast. Enjoy a café con leche (coffee with milk) and a tostada con tomate (toasted bread with tomato) at a café in the city center.

  - Visit the Alcazaba: From the café, head to the Alcazaba, a Moorish fortress that dates back to the 11th century. The entrance is near the city center, easily reachable by foot. Explore its lush gardens and enjoy panoramic views of the city. Admission is around €3.50, and it opens at 9:00 AM.

  - Explore Malaga Cathedral: A short walk from the Alcazaba, visit the Malaga Cathedral, known as "La Manquita" due to its unfinished right tower. Marvel at its stunning Renaissance and Baroque architecture. Entry costs approximately €6, and it provides a rich historical context of Malaga's Christian past.

- Afternoon:

- Lunch in Plaza de la Merced: Head to Plaza de la Merced for lunch. This lively square offers numerous dining options where you can try local specialties like espetos (sardines skewered and grilled over a wood fire) and Malaga salad.

- Picasso Museum Visit: After lunch, visit the Picasso Museum, just a short walk from Plaza de la Merced. It houses an impressive collection of Pablo Picasso's works, as he was born in Malaga. Admission is around €9, and it's a must-visit for art lovers.

- Stroll Around Calle Larios: Spend some time wandering through Calle Larios, the main shopping street. It's perfect for picking up souvenirs and experiencing the bustling local life.

- Evening:

  - Dinner at a Chiringuito: For dinner, go to one of Malaga's famous beachside restaurants, known as chiringuitos. Try local seafood dishes such as fried fish or paella.

  - Sunset at Malagueta Beach: Conclude your day with a stroll along Malagueta Beach, watching the sunset over the Mediterranean. It's a relaxing end to a busy day.

  - Nightcap in Centro Histórico: If you still have energy, finish your day with a drink in the Centro Histórico, where you can find numerous bars offering everything from local wines to craft beers.

Tips for Visitors:

- Comfortable Footwear: Wear comfortable shoes as Malaga's historic center is best explored on foot.

- Stay Hydrated: Keep hydrated, especially after midday, as Malaga can be warm, especially in the summer months.

- Public Transport: Utilize the city's efficient bus system if you prefer not to walk long distances. Buses are frequent, and a single ride costs around €1.30.

- Reservations: Consider making reservations for dinner, especially if you're dining at popular chiringuitos or during peak tourist seasons.

This packed day in Malaga offers a snapshot of its rich culture and vibrant lifestyle, making it an unforgettable part of your travels.

3 Days in Malaga

With three days in Malaga, you can delve deeper into the city's culture, explore more extensively, and even relax by the sea. This itinerary balances historical sightseeing with leisure activities to give you a comprehensive Malaga experience.

- Day 1: Explore Malaga's Historical Heart

    - Morning:

        - Breakfast in the City: Start your day at a local café with a café con leche and pan con tomate.

        - Visit Malaga Cathedral: Spend your morning at the Malaga Cathedral, appreciating its architectural beauty.

- Alcazaba and Roman Theatre: Explore these ancient ruins located close to each other, delving into Malaga's Moorish and Roman past.

- Afternoon:

    - Lunch in the Old Town: Enjoy lunch at a tapas bar in the old town, trying dishes like boquerones and albóndigas.

    - Picasso Museum: Discover the works of Pablo Picasso and learn about his connection to Malaga.

- Evening:

    - Dinner by the Port: Dine at Muelle Uno, a modern part of the port with restaurants overlooking the sea.

    - Night Walk and Ice Cream: Stroll along the Paseo del Parque and grab an ice cream from one of the local gelaterias.

- Day 2: Day of Leisure and Exploration

    - Morning:

        - Breakfast at the Hotel: Have a leisurely breakfast at your hotel.

        - Montes de Malaga Natural Park: Spend the morning hiking or enjoying a leisurely walk in this beautiful natural reserve close to the city.

- Afternoon:
    - Lunch in the Mountains: Enjoy lunch at a traditional venta (inn) in the mountains, where you can try rustic, home-cooked Andalusian food.
    - Gibralfaro Castle: In the afternoon, visit the Castillo de Gibralfaro for stunning views of Malaga and learn about its military history.
- Evening:
    - Tapas Tour: Join a tapas tour in the evening to experience different bars in the historic center, a perfect way to explore local cuisine and culture.

- Day 3: Relaxation and Modern Culture
    - Morning:
        - La Malagueta Beach: Start your day with a relaxed morning at Malagueta Beach, soaking up the sun and enjoying the Mediterranean.
    - Afternoon:
        - Lunch at Chiringuito: Have lunch at one of the beachside chiringuitos, trying fresh seafood like espetos de sardinas.
        - Centre Pompidou Malaga: Visit this branch of the famous Parisian museum to see contemporary art exhibits.

- Evening:
    - Farewell Dinner in Pedregalejo: Spend your last evening in Malaga in the fisherman's quarter of Pedregalejo, enjoying dinner at a seafront restaurant.
    - Nightcap in El Palo: End your trip with a nightcap at a local bar in the nearby El Palo neighborhood, mingling with locals.

Tips for Visitors:

- Transport Options: Consider a daily transport pass if planning multiple trips across the city—it's cost-effective and convenient.
- Book in Advance: Make reservations for popular attractions like the Picasso Museum to avoid long queues.
- Stay Protected: Bring sunscreen and a hat for your day out, especially at the beach or while hiking.

This three-day itinerary allows you to fully immerse yourself in Malaga's vibrant life and beautiful settings, providing a mix of historical insights, cultural experiences, and relaxation by the Mediterranean.

7 Days Exploring Costa del Sol

If you have a week to spend in the region, this comprehensive 7-day itinerary helps you explore the diverse attractions of Costa del Sol, from bustling beach resorts to quiet mountain villages. Malaga serves as a great base, but you'll also have the chance to venture further along the coast and into the Andalusian countryside.

- Day 1: Discover Malaga
  - Morning:
    - Start with a hearty breakfast at a local café. Enjoy churros with chocolate or a Spanish omelette.
    - Visit Malaga Cathedral and explore the surrounding historic center.
  - Afternoon:
    - Have lunch in the bustling Atarazanas Market, trying local specialties.
    - Visit the Picasso Museum and stroll through the nearby streets.
  - Evening:
    - Dine at a restaurant in the city center, trying tapas like gambas al pil pil (spicy garlic prawns).
    - Enjoy a Flamenco show at a local tablao.
- Day 2: Marbella and Puerto Banus
  - Morning:
    - Drive to Marbella (about an hour from Malaga). Explore the Old Town (Casco Antiguo) with its narrow streets and boutiques.
  - Afternoon:

- Lunch at a beachside chiringuito in Marbella.
- Spend the afternoon at Puerto Banus, watching luxury yachts and browsing designer shops.

- Evening:
  - Dinner in Puerto Banus overlooking the Mediterranean.
  - Return to Malaga or enjoy the nightlife in Marbella.

- Day 3: Ronda
  - Morning:
    - Travel to Ronda, one of Andalusia's most picturesque towns.
    - Explore the town, including the famous Puente Nuevo bridge spanning the deep gorge.
  - Afternoon:
    - Visit the Ronda bullring and its museum.
    - Enjoy lunch with views of the surrounding mountains.
  - Evening:
    - Return to Malaga, stopping at a local winery on the way for a tasting.

- Day 4: Nerja and Frigiliana

- Morning:
    - Drive to Nerja and visit the Nerja Caves, famous for their prehistoric paintings and natural formations.
- Afternoon:
    - Lunch in Nerja. Try fresh seafood like grilled squid.
    - Visit Frigiliana, a beautiful white-washed village nearby.
- Evening:
    - Dinner in Frigiliana at a restaurant with a view of the sea.
    - Return to Malaga.
- Day 5: Mijas
    - Morning:
        - Visit Mijas, a traditional Andalusian white village. Explore its cobbled streets and craft shops.
    - Afternoon:
        - Enjoy a traditional Andalusian lunch in Mijas.
        - Relax in the public gardens or take a donkey taxi tour around the village.

- Evening:
    - Return to Malaga for dinner and perhaps a quiet evening stroll along the beach.
- Day 6: Gibraltar
    - Full Day:
        - Take a day trip to Gibraltar. Visit the Rock of Gibraltar, meet the resident Barbary macaques, and explore the Great Siege Tunnels.
        - Lunch in Gibraltar, trying some British specialties alongside local dishes.
        - Return to Malaga in the evening.
- Day 7: Leisure Day in Malaga
    - Morning:
        - Enjoy a relaxed morning at Malagueta Beach.
    - Afternoon:
        - Last-minute shopping in Malaga's city center. Visit local markets for souvenirs.
        - Late lunch or early dinner at a beachside restaurant to enjoy the sunset.
    - Evening:

- Reflect on your journey with a peaceful evening walk by the port or a final night out enjoying Malaga's nightlife.

Tips for Visitors:

- Car Rental: Consider renting a car for flexibility in exploring distant locations like Ronda and Gibraltar.

- Accommodations: You might stay in Malaga throughout or book a few nights in other towns for less travel.

- Packing Essentials: Bring comfortable walking shoes, sunscreen, and a hat. A light jacket may be needed for cooler evenings.

This itinerary not only highlights the vibrant culture and stunning landscapes of Costa del Sol but also immerses you in the deep history and leisurely pace of southern Spain.

RESOURCES

Useful Websites and Apps

For travelers who want to navigate Malaga seamlessly and enrich their travel experience, here is a list of highly recommended websites and apps. These digital tools offer a wealth of information and practical features to help you plan your trip, explore like a local, and manage travel logistics efficiently.

Websites

1. Visit Malaga (visitmalaga.com)

- Purpose: Official tourism website of Malaga, providing comprehensive details on attractions, events, and essential visitor information.

- Features: Interactive maps, event calendars, and booking options for tours and tickets.

2. Renfe (renfe.com)

- Purpose: Official website for Spain's national railway, useful for booking train tickets and checking schedules.

- Features: Route planners, fare comparisons, and real-time updates on train services.

3. Andalucia.com

- Purpose: A resource for extensive cultural, historical, and practical information about Andalucia, including Malaga.

- Features: Regional insights, suggested itineraries, and local dining guides.

4. El Tiempo (eltiempo.es)

- Purpose: Provides detailed weather forecasts for Malaga and the Costa del Sol.

- Features: Hourly weather updates, 14-day forecasts, and climate statistics.

Apps

5. Malaga Official Guide

- Platform: Available on iOS and Android

- Purpose: The official app for Malaga tourism, offering guidance on exploring the city.

- Features: Offline maps, augmented reality, and a guide to the city's top attractions and restaurants.

6. Moovit

- Platform: Available on iOS and Android

- Purpose: An app to navigate public transport in Malaga with ease.

- Features: Real-time transit schedules, step-by-step navigation, and service alerts.

7. TripAdvisor

- Platform: Available on iOS and Android

- Purpose: Offers traveler reviews and recommendations on accommodations, eateries, and attractions.

- Features: User-generated content, booking tools, and travel forums.

8. SpanishDict

- Platform: Available on iOS and Android

- Purpose: An essential tool for travelers needing translations between Spanish and English.

- Features: Voice recognition for pronunciation help, verb conjugator, and a dictionary.

9. XE Currency Converter

- Platform: Available on iOS and Android

- Purpose: Helps manage currency conversions and track exchange rates.

- Features: Live currency rates and historical charts.

10. EatWith

- Platform: Available on iOS and Android

- Purpose: Connects you with local hosts in Malaga for an authentic dining experience.

- Features: Browse and book meals, cooking classes, and food tours hosted by locals.

Using These Tools: Before your trip, familiarize yourself with these websites and apps. Download the apps that fit your needs, and bookmark or create accounts on relevant websites. This preparation will enable you to access valuable information and services right at your fingertips, making your travel in Malaga and surrounding areas more enjoyable and hassle-free.

Emergency Contacts

When traveling to a new city like Malaga, it's crucial to be prepared for any unexpected situations by having a list of emergency contacts readily accessible. This section provides you with essential numbers and addresses to ensure your safety and well-being during your visit.

Emergency Numbers

1. General Emergency (112)

- Purpose: Use this number for any urgent assistance, including medical emergencies, fires, or crimes. It is the equivalent of 911 and can be dialed free of charge from any phone.
- Languages: Operators speak multiple languages, including English and Spanish.

2. National Police (091)

- Purpose: Contact the national police for issues related to crimes such as theft or assault.
- Note: For non-urgent police reports, look for a local police station to file a report in person.

3. Local Police (092)

- Purpose: Ideal for local issues such as minor accidents, noise complaints, or problems on local roads.

- Note: Local police are also helpful in situations where you might need assistance related to local laws and regulations.

4. Medical Emergencies (061)

- Purpose: Direct line to medical emergency services, specifically for ambulance and emergency medical care.

- Note: Use this number if you need immediate medical attention.

5. Fire Brigade (080)

- Purpose: For reporting fires or major accidents requiring the fire service.

- Note: This number can also be used for rescues and emergency situations involving hazardous materials.

Important Addresses

6. Hospitals:

- Hospital Regional de Málaga (also known as Hospital Carlos Haya)
    - Address: Av. Carlos Haya, 29010 Málaga, Spain
    - Phone: +34 951 03 00 00
    - Services: Full-service hospital with emergency department.

- Hospital Quirónsalud Málaga

    - Address: Calle Imperio Argentina, 1, 29004 Málaga, Spain

    - Phone: +34 952 17 71 00

    - Services: Private hospital offering a wide range of medical services including emergencies.

7. Pharmacies:

- For non-emergency medical needs, pharmacies are a good first stop.

- 24-Hour Pharmacy:

    - Farmacia Internacional

    - Address: Alameda Principal, 3, 29001 Málaga, Spain

    - Phone: +34 952 22 18 34

    - Services: Offers round-the-clock service for prescription and over-the-counter medications.

Additional Tips

- Embassy or Consulate Information: If you are a foreign visitor, it's wise to know the location and contact details of your country's embassy or consulate. They can provide assistance in case of lost passports or other legal difficulties.

- Keep a written copy of these contacts with you, as well as having them saved in your phone. This ensures you have access to them even if your phone is lost or its battery is depleted.

- Ask your hotel or host for local emergency numbers or additional contacts specific to the area you are staying in.

Being equipped with these emergency contacts will help you respond swiftly and efficiently to any unexpected situations, ensuring a safer travel experience in Malaga.

Printed in Great Britain
by Amazon